America's #1

Crafts
Magazine

Celebrate!
Holiday Crafts Throughout the Year

CREATIVE
PUBLISHING
international

Table of Contents

Thanksgiving

Hanukkah

Christmas

Celebrate! Created by: The Editors of Creative Publishing international, Inc. in cooperation with *Crafts Magazine* – PRIMEDIA Special Interest Publications.

President: Iain Macfarlane
Group Director, Book Development: Zoe Graul
Director, Creative Development: Lisa Rosenthal
Executive Managing Editor: Elaine Perry

Project Manager: Tracy Stanley
Senior Art Director: Mark Jacobson
Project Editor: Deborah Howe
Copy Editor: Janice Cauley
Illustrator: Earl R. Slack
Desktop Publishing Specialist: Laurie Kristensen
Print Production Manager: Patt Sizer

President & CEO Steven R. Elzy
Vice President, General Manager Harry Sailer
Editor Miriam Olson
Associate Editor Kim Shimkus
Assistant Editors Miriam Hughbanks
Amy Koepke
Sherrill Kolvek
Doris Roland
Administrative Assistant Diane Littlejohn
Art Director Dena L. Jenkins
Designers Sarah McClanahan
Barb Spink

ISBN 0-86573-185-3 (HC)

Printed on American paper by: World Color Press
02 01 00 99 / 5 4 3 2 1

Creative Publishing international, Inc. offers a
variety of how-to books. For information write:
Creative Publishing international, Inc.
 Subscriber Books
5900 Green Oak Drive
Minnetonka, MN 55343

*C*lay formed over foam balls becomes spheres that are the canvas for many designs—textured, marbled, grooved, written and painted—that can be adapted to any holiday or special occasion.

List of Materials

For 4 spheres

- 12″ (30.5 cm) square rolling cloth, waxed paper or nonstick surface
- One 5-lb. (2.2 kg) box Mexican Pottery Clay*
- Styrofoam® balls: four 3″ (7.5 cm)
- Paintbrushes: 1″ (2.5 cm) sponge, No. 4 flat, liner

- Water-based polyurethane
- Acrylic craft paints: white, red, royal blue, green, red, gold and silver, iridescent glitter
- Stencils: small flower and snowflake design
- Miscellaneous items: steak knife, masking tape, plastic wrap, ruler, rolling pin, small sponges, water container, craft

knife, fan, scissors, string, old small paintbrush, pencil, clay molding tools or stylus, sandpaper, toothpick, paint palette, soft cloths

*(See Sources on page 175 for purchasing information.)

1 *Preparation:* Tape rolling cloth to smooth work surface. Use steak knife to cut clay into four ³/₈" (1 cm) slices. Wrap foam balls tightly in plastic wrap; tape edges down smooth.

2 *Molding:* Work 1 slice in hands to soften; lay flat on cloth. Roll out clay to a ¼" (6 mm) thickness, peel from cloth, and wrap around foam as seen in the Step 2 illustration. Cover ball completely with an even thickness; cut away excess. Use damp sponge and water to smooth; however, clay is water-soluble and too much water will break it down. Roll sphere on surface and between hands to smooth and round.

3 *Cutting Line:* Wrap a piece of string around the sphere middle; pull tight to cut through the clay. Cut carefully through the plastic wrap only with a craft knife. Mark a notch across cutting line; see Step 6 illustration. Place sphere in front of a fan for 30 min.; rotate every 10 min. to harden on all sides.

4 *Decorating:* Trace desired pattern, such as Valentine heart, onto sphere. Use stylus or pencil to mark holes along the traced line. Roll out extra clay to desired thickness; trace heart onto clay. Cut out with steak knife; smooth edges with damp sponge. Score wrong side of heart and sphere surface with fork, and apply slip liberally to the scored areas with a small paintbrush. Make slip, which acts like glue, of 3 tbsp. (50 mL) clay and 1 tbsp. (15 mL) water in a small bowl; mix to a pastelike consistency.

5 *Unmolding:* Let sphere dry in front of fan, rotating every 30 min., for 1½ hrs. Gently ease clay sphere halves, but not the plastic, from foam; rest cut edge on surface. Continue drying

and rotating in front of fan for another 2 hrs. Remove the plastic, and let dry in front of fan overnight.

6 *Joining:* Make ⅛" (3 mm) ropes from extra clay by rolling between hands. Sand off any rough spots along the cut edges, and apply slip liberally. See the Step 6 illustration to place sphere halves together, matching the notches and working the clay ropes between them. Smooth the seam with damp sponge or thumbs; fill in any spots with slip. Use craft knife to trim off any excess clay; work between wet hands to smooth. Poke a hole in the bottom of sphere through soft clay with a toothpick to aid in drying. Rotate and dry in front of fan for 4 days.

7 *Paint Preparation:* Sand sphere smooth; use soft brush to remove sanding dust. Use sponge brush to coat the sphere with polyurethane; let dry for 2 hours. Let sphere dry between paint coats and colors. Use sponge brush to apply a basecoat of white; this prevents the clay color from showing through. Apply 2 coats: Valentine's Day, red; New Year's, gold; Christmas, royal blue; and Easter, white.

8 *Finishing:* Use flat brush to paint heart gold, as shown in the Step 8 illustration. Stencil silver snowflakes on Christmas sphere; paint with iridescent glitter all over. Stencil red tulips and green leaves on Easter sphere. Roughly dab red, green and blue paint randomly over New Year's ball; use liner brush to paint message in blue. Use damp sponge to apply gold over spheres; rub with a soft cloth to look like marbling. If desired, sand to achieve an aged look.

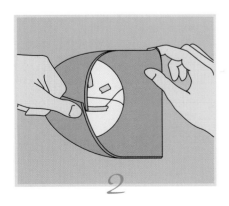

2

Matching notch

Matching notch

6

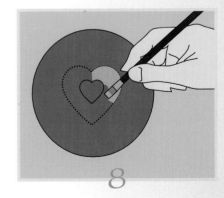

8

A New Year's Celebration wouldn't be complete without lights and glitz, glamour and glow. These candles are quick and easy ways to make your house look as festive as the occasion deserves.

List of Materials

For Ice Luminaries

- Plastic bucket, such as 1-gallon (3.8 L) ice cream container
- Plastic jar, such as empty mayonnaise or peanut butter jar
- Votive or short pillar candle

For Star Candle

- 3-wick white candle, 6" (15 cm) high and 6" (15 cm) diameter
- 60 each sequins: small silver, large blue and silver
- 120 sequin pins, 3/4" (2 cm) long
- Glittered glass candle stand or plate, 6" (15 cm) diameter
- Miscellaneous items: rocks, dish or hand towel, 3 bowls, new pencil with fresh eraser, ruler

Ice Luminaries

1 *Forming:* Center plastic jar, and place at the bottom of the 1-gallon (3.8 L) bucket. Place rocks in the jar to weight it. Fill the bucket with water, as shown in the Step 1 illustration, up to the rim of the jar. Place the bucket outdoors, or in a freezer, until the water is frozen. Remove the rocks from the jar.

2 *Unmolding:* Pour warm water into the jar to release it from the ice; let it set for about 1 minute and remove jar. Wrap the bucket with a warm, wet towel to release ice from bucket. Place candle into the hole created by the jar.

3 *Deep Buckets:* Fill bucket partway with water; surface of water should be below rim of the bucket a distance greater than the height of the candle you will use in the luminary. Freeze water. Follow Steps 1 and 2 above to complete the luminary, centering the jar in the bucket on the ice.

4 *Use:* Use ice luminaries to line driveways and walkways, or add interest to a backyard view by clustering several on a patio, deck or stairs. See the Step 4 illustration for how to make a holiday arrangement by placing ice luminaries in large planters and surrounding them with sprigs of evergreen and berries. Ice luminaries can be used as long as the temperature remains below freezing. Brush the snow off the candles periodically, and spray the ice formation with water to return the ice to its clear state. For long-burning luminaries, use pillar candles, rather than votive candles.

Star Candle

1 *Sequins:* Place the sequin pins, and the small and large sequins, each in a separate bowl. Place the candle on a flat work surface. Take a sequin pin and put it through the center hole in a sequin. Push the sequin pin lightly into the candle with your thumb, just to hold it from falling out. Use the eraser end of a new pencil, as shown in the Step 1 illustration, to push the sequin pin all the way into the candle.

2 *Finishing:* Repeat the process, placing the small and large sequins randomly over the candle surface about ½" (1.3 cm) apart. Leave at least a ½" (1.3 cm) margin free of sequins along the top and bottom candle edge, because the pressure of pushing a sequin pin in may cause the candle to crack along the edges. Place the candle on the candle stand; sprinkle additional sequins and decorations around the base and on the table. Never leave a lit candle unattended.

This is the perfect gift for the person who has a little trouble remembering those special dates. It also is a great day brightener, with every glance finding a friendly face and fun events that recently passed or, better yet, are coming up in the days ahead.

List of Materials

- Wall or desktop calendar
- Colored and metallic markers
- Photos that you can cut up

- Decorative items: stickers, rubber stamps, rub-on transfers, rub-on letters (These items, and many more, can be found in the memory book or scrapbook sections of craft stores.)

- Confetti and sequins
- Miscellaneous items: ruler, glue stick

8

1 *Preparation:* This is a very extensive and ultra organized approach to a personalized calendar. Let how well you know the person, and how detailed he or she is, guide you as to how detailed you make the calendar.

2 *Holidays:* Check to see that the purchased calendar has all the traditional holidays marked. List other pertinent holidays that the calendar owner will celebrate, based on religion, culture and lifestyle. If the calendar owner has school-age children in his or her life, get a copy of their school calendar.

3 *People:* Make a list of important people and pets in the calendar owner's life: spouse, children, parents, friends, bosses, teachers, coaches, aunts, uncles, etc. Make a list of important dates regarding each important person. These could be very diverse, and will depend upon the relationship. Some possibilities are: birthday, anniversary, graduation, christening, adoption, beginning or end of relationship (first date or divorce), vacations, camp dates for children, weddings, family reunions. For birthdays and anniversaries, record the year to figure the person's age or which anniversary it is.

4 *Events:* Make a list of the calendar owner's interests: hobbies, sports, organizations, pastimes, volunteer efforts, classes, etc. Find out dates associated with those interests, such as: the meeting or class schedule for community ed, church, local food shelf or library volunteer group; the season opening and close dates for fishing, hunting, football, hockey, theater, orchestra; suggested tilling, planting, fertilizing dates for a gardener; event and fundraiser dates for museums, civic groups, schools, etc.

5 *Master List:* Take all the lists from above and make a chronological list, as shown in the Step 5 illustration, grouping them by month. Review the list for duplicate events on a date. If necessary, decide which event is most important and plan on putting only 1 event on the calendar. If room permits, put more than 1 item on a date on the calendar.

6 *Decorating:*
Wall Calendar with Photos: Take any photos you have of the people (or any pets) on the list, and cut and trim them to fit the calendar space. Lay them out a month at a time. Glue them onto the calendar with the glue stick. Embellish the actual date with colored markers and stickers. Markers and confetti or sequins can also decorate holidays, such as shown for New Year's.
Weekly Desk Calendar: Hand-write in the event on the date with colored markers; decorate with stickers or freehand drawings. If you don't hand-write well, mark the event with rubber stamps, stickers and rub-on letters; see the Step 6 illustration.
Daily Desk Calendar: Mark an event such as a Memorial Day Camping Trip with stickers or rubber stamps. No words are necessary for special occasions; remember, "A picture is worth a thousand words!"

7 *Finishing:* Wrap the calendar in a box, being sure to include extra stickers and markers, so the recipient can add in events and update the calendar as the year progresses. For a clever wrapping idea, use old calendar pages for wrapping paper, or solid-color paper with dates, days of the week and months of the year written all over it; see the Step 7 illustration.

New Year!   New Year!   New Year!   New Year!   New Year!   New Year!

FLORAL
Shadow Box

For a lovely Valentine's message that will become a keepsake, make this shadow box by gluing greeting cards and dried florals in a box that you have decoupaged with pretty paper.

List of Materials

- Two 10.75" x 2.3" x 7.25" (27.4 x 5.8 x 18.7 cm) wooden boxes with lids, or similar size*
- 1 yd. (0.95 cm) wrapping paper with rose motif
- Glues: decoupage, hot glue gun, glue stick
- 1" (2.5 cm) sponge brush
- 2¼ yd. (2.1 m) gold foil paper trim, ½" (1.3 cm) wide
- 8½" x 11" (21.8 x 28 cm) sheets copier paper: 3 marbled pink, 3 white

- Computer or black and white photocopy machine, optional
- 1 greeting card or photo, 2 sentimental messages—computer-generated, photo-copied, hand-lettered, rub-on transfers, etc.
- 6 dimensional self-adhesive circle photo mounts, ¼" (6 mm) diameter
- Dried or preserved naturals: 6-8 nigella pods, 12 nigella orientalis, 36 miniature roses,

- 6-8 burgundy straw flowers, small bunch each of: poa, blue and purple larkspur, lavender everlastings, natural ivory lace, white and purple statice*
- 2 gold hinges with screws, 1" (2.5 cm) long
- Miscellaneous items: screwdriver, ruler, pencil, scissors

*(See Sources on pg. 175 for purchasing information.)

1 *Decoupage Paper:* Use screwdriver to pry factory-installed hinges off the boxes. Set aside the lids; use the 2 box bases only. Place wrinkle-free wrapping paper on flat work surface. Thin wrapping paper could possibly have more wrinkles while decoupaging; stiffer wrapping paper will work best with fewer wrinkles and cleaner folds.

2 *Marking Paper:* Place box on the wrapping paper; measure the outside height of the box with a ruler. Mark a margin around the box on each side equal to the box height, as shown in the Step 2A illustration. Continue the margin lines on each side to create a corner square as shown. Repeat for the other box; cut out both rectangles along the marked lines. Cut out diamond shape from each corner square as shown in Step 2B.

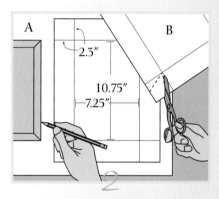

3 *Decoupaging Box Exterior Base:* Follow manufacturer's instructions to apply decoupage glue to the bottom of the box with sponge brush. Let decoupage glue dry between coats. Place paper right side down on table, place box on paper within marked lines, and press down. Turn box over, and smooth wrapping paper with fingers; work from the center outward.

4 *Decoupaging Box Exterior Sides:* Place box on its side, and fold 1 side edge of wrapping paper up, creasing gently. Apply decoupage glue to side, and gently press paper onto glue. Fold extra corner paper over, and glue onto the adjacent side for a corner overlap, as seen in the Step 4 illustration. Repeat folding and gluing for the adjacent side, trimming the corner even with the box edge. Repeat to continue gluing paper around the sides.

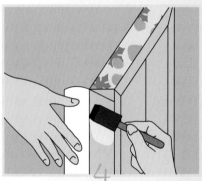

5 *Gold Trim:* Apply decoupage glue to 1 upper edge of box with sponge brush. Press the gold trim onto the glue. Wrap the trim around the corner, folding the extra paper into a diagonal miter. Continue folding and gluing around entire box, covering beginning spot. Cut trim, ending on a miter; see the Step 5 illustration. Let dry, wrap excess gold trim down, and burnish with the side of a pencil to make it lie flat.

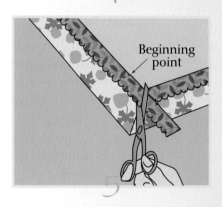

Beginning point

6 *Message & Image Layout:* Measure the inner box length and width; lightly mark with pencil onto 2 white copier paper sheets. Cut out image from a greeting card, or use a photo. Lay out message and image onto marked white paper to see how they fit. To make 3-D "joy," cut it out, enlarge it to about twice its original size; lay out on white paper. Trim and adjust layout until you are satisfied.

Continued

7 *Message & Image Creation:* Remove the image and enlarged "joy" from layout.

Hand Lettering or Rub–On Transfers: Mark inner box size from Step 6 onto 2 sheets of pink marbled paper. Make your message directly onto the paper following the layout; do enlarged "joy" on the third pink sheet.

Photocopying: Use glue stick to spot-glue message on the back side to the white paper. See the Step 7 illustration to leave a blank space in the message for the enlarged "joy." Place each white layout sheet in the photocopy machine, and copy onto a sheet of pink marbled paper. Photocopy "joy" onto the third sheet of pink.

Computer–Generated: Set up and print out on pink marbled paper within appropriate size area; print enlarged "joy" on a separate third sheet.

8 *Decoupaging Box Interior:* Cut out the pink paper along the inner box measurement marked lines. If lines did not come through during photocopying, re-mark lines. Apply decoupage glue to the inside bottom of box with sponge brush. Place pink paper inside, message side up, and press gently into glue.

9 *Three-Dimensional Cutouts:* Trim around "joy," leaving a 1/16" (1.5 mm) border; refer to the photo. Cut dimensional photo mount circles in half so they do not show on the front side of "joy"; adhere to back side of "joy." Remove paper backing and place "joy" on message where appropriate space was left; see the Step 9 illustration. Apply photo mounts in each corner of the image, remove paper backing, and adhere to left side of box where space was left.

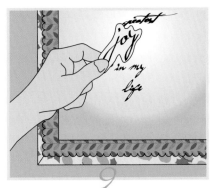

10 *Hinges:* Mark the box backs lightly with a pencil 2¾" (7 cm) in from each edge. Place boxes together; center hinges on the pencil marks. Use screwdriver to attach hinges to box.

11 *Florals:* Cut stems off the dried florals; use only the heads. Refer to the photo to hot-glue the florals in a single layer around the entire box inside. Glue larger items such as rosebuds, nigella, straw flowers and larkspur evenly around the box first; see the Step 11 illustration. Fill in with statice, poa, everlastings and ivory lace. Add more items to the corners to round them out. Add additional ivory lace, filling in and framing the messages.

JEWELED
Heart Pin

*C*raft this pin, reminiscent of a Victorian brooch, quickly with beads, jewels and cord on a wooden heart base.

List of Materials

- 3" (7.5 cm) wooden heart
- 1 pkg. each 10/0 rocaille beads: pink, royal blue
- 1 pkg. 4.5 mm black bugle beads
- 5 assorted round mounted jewels, 5/8" to 1" (1.5 to 2.5 cm)
- 1 yd. (0.95 m) gold tubular cord
- 1¼" (3.2 cm) pin back
- Gold acrylic craft paint
- 1" (2.5 cm) sponge brush
- Hot glue gun
- Miscellaneous items: tracing paper, pencil, ruler, scissors

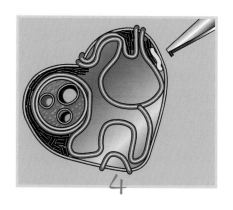

1 Painting: Use sponge brush and gold paint to paint the wooden heart on both the front and back sides, and the edges. Let dry; repeat for better coverage, if desired.

2 Large Jewel: Refer to photo for jewel and bead placement. Hot-glue the largest 1" (2.5 cm) jewel in the upper left section of the heart. Hot-glue a strip of gold cord around the large jewel.

3 Cord: Begin at the center top of the heart, and hot-glue cord around the outer edge. Cut cord and meet beginning cord at top center. Glue 1 end of cord to top of heart on the back side. Bring to the front and hot-glue in a squiggly free-form design on heart; end at beginning point on back. Cut 2½" (6.5 cm) of cord; hot-glue 1 end to lower left of heart on back side. Bring to front, make a loop, and glue end on the back.

4 Bugle Beads: Working in small sections, apply hot-glue and fill in with bugle beads; refer to the illustration. Place bugle beads around the large mounted jewel and small spots around the edges of the heart. Either sprinkle beads on the glue, and brush off after the glue hardens, or place beads as desired with a tweezer.

5 Finishing: Fill in remaining spaces with jewels and blue and pink rocaille beads. Hot-glue pin back onto back side of heart in center.

13

Valentine's Day   Valentine's Day   Valentine's Day   Valentine's Day

List of Materials

**For 1 Each Double Twist &
Single Twist Heart Ornaments**

- 1 pkg. 50 g each oven-bake
  modeling clay: white, pink

- Crystal heart with bail:
  18 mm pink, 10 mm clear

- Dried florals: 2 roses, glittered
  baby's breath, asparagus fern
  sprays

- Scrap of white net or tulle

- Clear monofilament thread

- Hot glue gun

- Miscellaneous items: nonstick
  baking sheet, toothpick, rolling
  pin, oven, scissors, ruler

Double Twist Heart

1 *Preparation:* Use ¼ pkg. each pink and white clay. Follow manu-facturer's instructions to knead each color until it feels warm, like smooth putty. Roll clay by hand until you have a long strand of each about 17″ (43 cm) long.

2 *Forming:* Pick up both pieces and match the ends. Twist them around each other in the air as shown in the Step 2 illustration, pressing slightly to adhere. Form clay on a nonstick baking sheet into a heart shape, approximately 4″ (10 cm) across. Press the ends together in the center V, and flatten.

3 *Baking:* Use toothpick to poke 2 vertical holes in the V, about 1″ (2.5 cm) apart; see the Step 3 illustration. Bake in the oven according to clay manufacturer's instructions, usually 20-30 min. until hardened in a 265°F (132°C) oven. Remove from oven; let cool completely on baking sheet.

4 *Hanger:* Hang clear crystal heart with monofilament thread from the lower hole so it hangs within the heart; see photo. Cut desired length of monofilament thread for ornament hanger. Thread through the upper hole, tie in an overhand knot, and trim thread ends.

5 *Florals:* Fold and hot-glue net or tulle to the front of the heart V for a base. Refer to the photo to hot-glue in order: asparagus fern, baby's breath and rose.

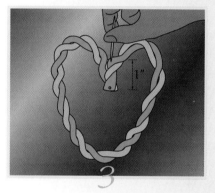

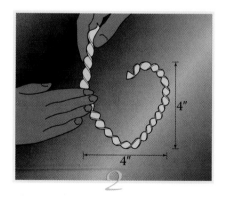

Single Twist Heart

1 *Preparation:* Use ½ pkg. white clay. Follow manufacturer's instruc-tions to knead clay until it feels warm, like smooth putty. Roll clay by hand until you have a long strand about 17″ (43 cm) long. Flatten with a rolling pin until it is about ⅛″ (3 mm) thick.

2 *Forming:* Carefully lift the clay strand up in the air and twist, referring to the photo. Form clay on a flat surface into a heart shape, approximately 4″ (10 cm) across; see the Step 2 illustration. Press the ends together in the center V, and flatten.

3 *Finishing:* Repeat Steps 3-5 of Double Twist Heart to complete, hanging pink crystal heart from the lower hole.

HEARTS APLENTY
Afghan

$\mathcal{U}$sing three shades of
yarn, a simple shell stitch is
worked in rows to form a
beautiful and fascinating
pattern of interlocking
hearts. Quick to stitch, this
colorful throw will wrap
someone special with love.

List of Materials

- 100% acrylic worsted-weight yarn, 3.5 oz. (90 g) skeins: 6 skeins pink; 5 skeins each: white and green
- Size J aluminum crochet hook
- Yarn needle
- Miscellaneous items: scissors, ruler

1 *Preparation:* Refer to the Crochet Stitches and Abbreviations on page 162.

Gauge: 1 shell = 1" (2.5 cm), 4 rows = 2" (5 cm)
Finished Size: Approximately 44" x 65" (112 x 165.5 cm)

2 *Shell Stitch:* In specified sp or st, work the pattern stitch [(dc, ch 1) 3 times, dc]. To change yarn colors, work last st of current color up through last pull-through of st. Drop current color to wrong side of work, pick up new color from wrong side of work, yo and draw through rem lps on hook.

3 *Afghan:* Ch 128 with J crochet hook and pink yarn.
Row 1: Sc in 2nd ch from hook and in each ch across; turn. (127 sts)
Row 2 (right side): Ch 3 (counts as first dc), sk next 2 sts, shell in next st, (sk next 4 sts, shell in next st) across to last 3 sts; end sk 2 sts, dc in last st. Fasten off. (25 shells)
Row 3: With right side facing, join white in top of beg ch-3 with a sl st, ch 4 (counts as first dc and ch 1), dc in same st, (sk next shell, shell in skipped sc of 2 rows below) across; end (dc, ch 1, dc) in last dc. Fasten off.
Row 4: With right side facing, join green in 3rd ch of beg ch-4 with a sl st, ch 3 (counts as first dc), (shell in center ch of next shell 2 rows below) across, dc in last dc. Fasten off.
Row 5: With right side facing, join pink in top of beg ch-3 with a sl st, ch 4 (counts as first dc and ch 1), dc in same st, (sk next shell, shell in center ch of next shell 2 rows below) across, end (dc, ch 1, dc) in last dc. Fasten off.
Rep Rows 4 and 5 using white, green, and pink in order until you reach 64" (163 cm), or 1" (2.5 cm) less than desired length, ending after working a Row 4.

4 *Border:* With right side facing, join pink with a sl st in top of ch-3 at beg of last row.
Rnd 1: Ch 1, 3 sc in same st, (2 sc in next ch-1 sp, sk next ch-1 sp, 2 sc in next ch-1 sp) across each shell, 3 sc in last dc; * working along the sides of the rows, sc evenly across to the next corner *, 3 sc in first ch of starting ch, sc in each ch across, 3 sc in last ch; rep from * to *; join with a sl st in first sc.
Rnd 2: Ch 3 (counts as first dc); *(2 dc, ch 2, 2 dc) in center sc of each 3-sc group, dc in each st to the next corner; rep from * around; join with a sl st in top of beg ch-3. Fasten off. Weave in yarn ends on wrong side of afghan with yarn needle.

CUPID'S
Photo Cube

A little love is in every pretty pink floss and metallic braid stitch taken on the plastic canvas, making this an extra-special gift to display candid shots of the one you love.

List of Materials

- 10-mesh plastic canvas, 1 sheet
- 6 skeins 6-strand DMC embroidery floss, Vy. Lt. Cranberry No. 605
- Heavy (No. 32) Kreinik metallic braid: 12 yd. (11.04 m) Star Pink No. 92; 8 yd. (7.35 m) Pale Pink No. 192
- No. 20 tapestry needle
- 2" (5 cm) white/pink lace appliqué
- 4 small photos
- 3¼" (8.2 cm) white lightweight cardboard squares, four
- Miscellaneous items: pencil, ruler, scissors, craft knife, emery board, white craft glue

1 *Preparation:* Refer to the Plastic Canvas Instruction and Stitches on page 159. Cut five 33-bar squares from plastic canvas. Follow the bold outlines on the Side Stitch Chart to cut out heart opening with craft knife on the 4 photo cube sides.

2 *Stitching:* Refer to the Stitch Charts; each line on the graph represents 1 bar of plastic canvas. Work Star Pink No. 92 braid continental stitches in a square along the top, and in rows on the sides. Overcast the heart openings on photo cube sides at the same time. Use 12 strands of embroidery floss Vy. Lt. Cranberry No. 605 to finish the top and sides with Gobelin stitches. Make sure to leave unstitched the 4 corners on all pieces, and the additional 4 squares on the top where the Pale Pink No. 192 braid stitches will go.

3 *Assembly:* Use Pale Pink No. 192 to overcast sides to the top, then sides together, filling in the above-mentioned corner squares. Overcast the bottom edges also. Trim photos to match cardboard squares. Spot-glue corners of photo to cardboard, then cardboard to inside stitched cube. Glue lace appliqué to center top.

Top Stitch Chart

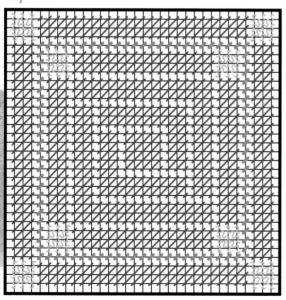

Side Stitch Chart

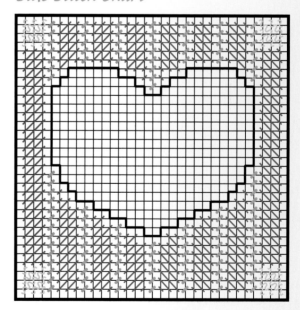

Cupid's Photo Cube Color Key

Symbol	#	Color
✎	092	Star Pink Continental
∿	192	Pale Pink Gobelin
╱	605	Lt. Cranberry Gobelin

Flowers for Valentine's Day are very traditional, especially roses, but this lovely bouquet is anything but traditional. It combines the simplicity of carnations with the elegance of roses in an expression of bright color and rich fragrances sure to please.

List of Materials

For Each Pot

- 6″ (15 cm) clay pot
- Saucer to fit clay pot
- Plastic liner to fit into clay pot, available from your local florist or craft store
- Acrylic craft paints: hot pink, bright yellow
- Two 1″ (2.5 cm) sponge brushes
- High-gloss spray finish
- 3″ x 4″ x 8″ (7.5 x 10 x 20.5 cm) brick wet arrangement floral foam
- Live florals, available from your local florist or craft store: 7 yellow roses; 10 standard hot pink carnations; 3 stems of tree fern, about 18″ (46 cm) tall
- Miscellaneous items: paint palette, newspaper, serrated knife, ruler, sharp knife, cutting board or surface, scissors

1 *Basecoating:* Let paints dry between each coat and each color. Use 1″ (2.5 cm) sponge brush to basecoat clay pot rim and saucer with yellow paint. Paint the saucer on both the top and bottom. Use the other sponge brush to basecoat the clay pot body with hot pink paint. Use as many coats as necessary for complete coverage, about 5 coats of yellow paint and 2 to 3 coats of pink paint.

2 *Glossy Finish:* Set up newspaper sheets outdoors or in a well-ventilated area. Follow the manufacturer's instructions to spray the pot and saucer with at least 2 coats of high-gloss spray finish; let dry overnight.

3 *Foam Base:* Soak floral foam in the sink for at least 30 minutes. Place foam in pot liner; use serrated knife to trim foam to fit in liner, cutting off the top of the foam level with the top of the liner. See the Step 3 illustration. Place the liner with the foam into the painted clay pot. Fill the pot with water.

4 *Carnation Border:* Use a sharp knife and a cutting surface to cut off the carnation stems, 1 at a time, to a 4″ (10 cm) length. Remove any leaves remaining on the stems. Place the carnations around the edge of the pot, pushing them into the foam at a slight angle. See the Step 4A illustration. Place all 10 of the carnations around the pot in a circle border; see 4B.

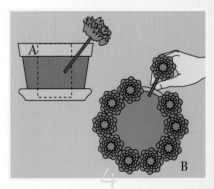

5 *Roses:* Use a sharp knife and a cutting surface to cut off the rose stems, 1 at a time, to a 4″ (10 cm) length. Remove any leaves remaining on the stems. Place the roses in 3 rows in the middle of the pot, as shown in the Step 5 illustration, pushing them straight down into the foam.

6 *Tree Ferns:* Use scissors to cut off small pieces of the tree ferns, about 2″ to 3″ (2.5 to 7.5 cm) tall. Push the pieces into the foam between each flower, until the floral foam can no longer be seen. Also place them in the foam in a circle around the top rim of the pot. Make sure to add water to the pot every day.

HEART SMART
Pinafore

*S*ew a practical and pretty pinafore for your favorite little girl from just four homespun towels, a doily and a yo-yo. Use it over a dress as shown, or keep it in the kitchen for baking and cooking lessons.

List of Materials

- 1 each homespun dish towels* 19" x 28" (48.5 x 71 cm): ecru stripe, ecru check, cranberry check, navy plaid
- 4" (10 cm) Battenberg star doily*
- 1½" (3.8 cm) navy premade yo-yo*
- 2 natural buttons, ¾" (2 cm)
- Fusible web, 9" x 11" (23 x 28 cm)
- Embroidery floss to match buttons, sewing needle
- Pattern Page 165
- Miscellaneous items: scissors, ruler, iron, sewing machine with feather stitch, matching threads, straight pins, disappearing-ink marker, tracing paper, pencil

*(See Sources on pg. 175 for purchasing information.)

Valentine's Day   Valentine's Day   Valentine's Day   Valentine's Day

1 *Front & Back:* Cut the ecru stripe dish towel in half to make two 14″ x 19″ (35.5 x 48.5 cm) rectangles. Turn the cut edges under ¼″ (6 mm) twice and stitch to hem.

2 *Shaping:* See the Step 2 illustration to shape the pinafore front and back. Follow the measurements to fold back the corners, and trim them off leaving a ¾″ (2 cm) seam allowance. Turn under the cut edges ¼″ (6 mm), then ½″ (1.3 cm) and topstitch.

3 *Tabs:* Cut one 4″ x 10″ (10 x 25.5 cm) strip each from the navy plaid and the cranberry check dish towels. Fold strip in half lengthwise and sew a ¼″ (6 mm) seam along the long edge; see the Step 3A illustration. Press the seam open and center it, as shown in the Step 3B illustration. Mark and sew the points on 1 end of each tie; trim the point seam, and turn right side out. Tuck in the open ends ¼″ (6 mm), and press.

4 *Ties:* Cut four 3¼″ x 19″ (8.2 x 48.5 cm) strips from the ecru check dish towel. Repeat Step 3 to stitch ties the same as tabs. See the Step 2 illustration and the photo for tie and tab placement; pin straight edges to the wrong side of the pinafore. Sew 2 ties to the pinafore front, and 2 ties and 2 tabs to the pinafore back.

5 *Heart:* Trace the patterns onto the paper side of fusible web. Follow the fusible web manufacturer's instructions to fuse the web to the dish towels as indicated on the patterns. Cut the 3 heart pieces from the fused dish towel fabric, and remove the paper backing. Refer to the photo and Step 5 illustration to place the heart on the pinafore front and fuse. Machine-stitch around the outside raw edges with a feather stitch and black thread.

6 *Finishing:* Pin the star doily on the navy plaid heart piece, and topstitch it in place. Tack the yo-yo in the center of the star. Pin the tabs to the pinafore front. Sew a button through the tabs and pinafore, using 6 strands of embroidery floss.

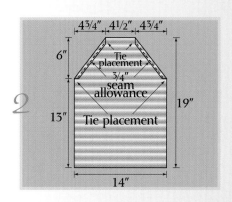

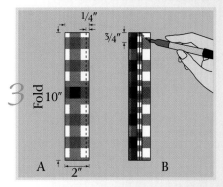

WILL YOU
Be Mine?

Pattern-blade scissors give a different twist to popular heart shapes, while pretty trims like heart candies and ribbon roses finish off these cards that say "Handmade with Love."

List of Materials

For Candy Heart Card

- Paper: 8½" x 11" (21.8 x 28 cm) pink, 4" x 8½" (10 x 21.8 cm) each purple and turquoise
- 7 candy hearts
- ½ yd. (0.5 m) pink rattail cord

For Button Card

- Paper: 8½" x 11" (21.8 x 28 cm) tan, 4" x 8½" (10 x 21.8 cm) brown and white, 4" (10 cm) square each red and lilac

- 7 assorted buttons
- A few strands natural raffia

For Ribbon Rose Card

- Paper: 8½" x 11" (21.8 x 28 cm) dark pink, 3" x 10" (7.5 x 25.5 cm) light pink, 3" (7.5 cm) square each lavender, light green, dark pink, light blue
- Light pink ribbon roses: four ¾" (2 cm) and one ½" (1.3 cm)

- 1 yd. (0.95 m) white satin ribbon, ⅛" (3 mm) thick

For All Cards

- Assorted pattern-blade scissors
- Glues: white craft glue, glue stick
- Miscellaneous items: tracing paper, pencil, ruler, scissors

24

For All Cards

General: Trace heart patterns to tracing paper with pencil. Cut all paper out with pattern–blade scissors. Use glue stick for gluing paper, and white craft glue for the trims and embellishments. Refer to photo for decoration placement.

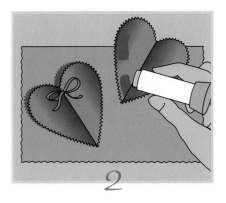

Candy Heart Card

1 *Cutting:* Fold 8¹/2" x 11" (21.8 x 28 cm) pink sheet in half to make an 8¹/2" x 5¹/2" (21.8 x 14 cm) card; trim edges. Cut 2 large hearts from purple paper and 5 medium hearts from turquoise paper.

2 *Gluing:* Cut pink rattail cord in half, make into 2 bows, and glue onto outside fold of purple hearts. Refer to the illustration to glue purple hearts to card with fold up, gluing on heart point and curves. Glue turquoise hearts to card along the fold only. Glue candy hearts to card as desired.

Button Card

1 *Cutting:* Fold 8¹/2" x 11" (21.8 x 28 cm) tan sheet in half to make an 8¹/2" x 5¹/2" (21.8 x 14 cm) card; trim all edges of tan and brown paper. Cut 1 large heart and 2 small hearts from white paper, 1 medium heart from red paper and 1 medium and 1 small heart from lilac paper.

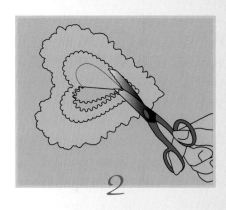

2 *Gluing:* Glue brown sheet at an angle on front of tan card. Glue red heart to center of large white heart and 1 small white heart to center of medium lilac heart. See the illustration to trace the small heart pattern to the center of the lilac/white heart, and cut it out. Glue hearts onto card. Cut raffia in half, make into 2 bows and glue onto card. Glue buttons to card as desired.

Ribbon Rose Card

1 *Cutting:* Fold 8¹/2" x 11" (21.8 x 28 cm) dark pink sheet in half to make a 4¹/4" x 11" (10.8 x 28 cm) card; trim all edges of dark pink and pink paper. Cut 1 medium heart each from lavender, light green, dark pink and light blue paper, plus 1 small heart from light blue.

2 *Gluing:* Glue light pink sheet centered on front of card. Glue hearts to card starting with the lavender heart at the top. Cut white satin ribbon into 5 pieces and make into bows. Glue bows, then ribbon roses onto hearts.

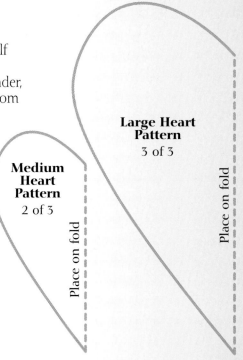

Large Heart Pattern
3 of 3

Place on fold

Medium Heart Pattern
2 of 3

Place on fold

Small Heart Pattern
1 of 3

Place on fold

AMISH HEARTS
Quilt

Vibrant colors lend drama to the simple repeating heart design in this mock quilt done by tucking fabric pieces into a foam base.

List of Materials

- 24" (61 cm) Styrofoam® square, 1" (2.5 cm) thick
- 45" (115 cm) cotton fabrics: 1¼ yd. (1.15 m) black; ¼ yd. (0.25 m) each: dark turquoise, red; ⅛ yd. (0.15 m) each: light turquoise, purple, lavender
- 1" (2.5 cm) sawtooth hanger

- Pattern Page 170
- Miscellaneous items: serrated knife, candle stub, yardstick, tracing paper, pencil, fine-point felt marker, scissors, rotary cutter and mat, putty knife, white craft glue

1 *Base:* Wax the serrated knife blade with candle stub, hold knife perpendicular to cutting line, and use a sawing motion to cut foam to a 23½" (59.8 cm) square. Smooth rough edges with a scrap piece of foam. Refer to the Scoring and Assembly Guide. Use the marker and yardstick to draw the design on 1 side of the foam. Score all the lines with a sharp pencil.

2 *Fabrics:* Wash and dry fabrics, if desired; press out all wrinkles. Trace the 3 patterns, and cut out. Cut fabrics as indicated on the patterns. In addition, cut the following:

8 red strips, 2¼" x 5¼" (6 x 13.2 cm)

2 dark turquoise strips, 2¼" x 17½" (6 x 44.3 cm)

2 dark turquoise strips, 2¼" x 20½" (6 x 52.3 cm)

23¾" (60.4 cm) black square for backing

4 black strips, 2¼" x 8¼" (6 x 21.2 cm)

2 black strips, 4½" x 20½" (11.5 x 52.3 cm)

2 black strips, 4½" x 27½" (11.5 x 69.8 cm)

2¼" (6 cm) squares: 8 each lavender and light turquoise, 4 each red and dark turquoise, 13 purple

3 *Tucking:* Center a purple square over the center square on the foam. See the Step 3 illustration to hold the putty knife perpendicular to the foam and tuck the seam allowances into the scored lines. Trim the excess fabric with scissors, being careful not to cut the tucked fabric. Tuck in any stray fabric edges with serrated knife tip. Repeat, working from the center outward, to tuck fabric into the foam to make the 4 center hearts.

4 *Borders:* Tuck the shorter dark turquoise strips, then the longer. Repeat for the black strips, leaving a ½" (1.3 cm) seam allowance along the outer edge. Fold the seam allowance to the back side, and glue.

5 *Finishing:* Press under ¼" (6 mm) along all edges of the black backing square. Center on the back of the foam, and glue. Glue the sawtooth hanger centered on the back of 1 side or diagonally across a corner, 1" (2.5 cm) in from the edge.

Amish Hearts Quilt Scoring & Assembly Guide

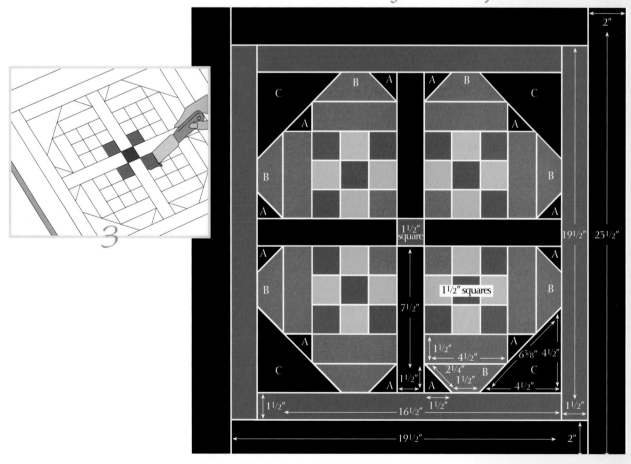

BUTTERFLY
Pincushion

*S*how where your heart is for Valentine's Day with this splendid pincushion. Rayon embroidery floss adds a sleek elegance to the cross-stitched blue butterflies sipping nectar from pink clover blossoms.

List of Materials

- 14-count blush Aida cloth, 9¹/₂" (24.3 cm) square

- 6-strand DMC rayon embroidery floss: 1 skein each of colors listed on Color Key

- No. 24 tapestry needle

- 2 yd. (1.85 m) pale peach wire-edge ribbon, 1¹/₂" (3.8 cm) wide

- Polyester fiberfill, 8 oz. (250 g)

- 1" (2.5 cm) plastic ring

- Miscellaneous items: scissors, ruler, sewing machine and matching thread

Butterfly Pincushion Stitch Chart

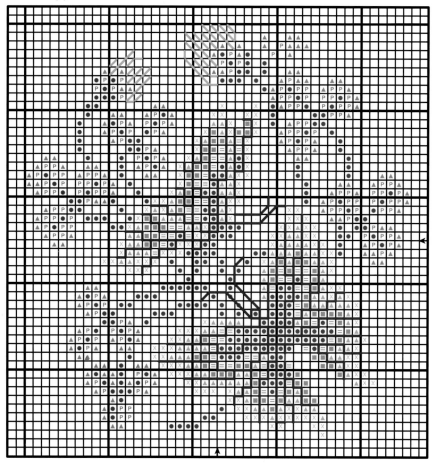

1 *Design Placement:* Fold the Aida cloth in half twice. Finger-press the creases; unfold. Find the center of the bottom right square. Mark with a temporary stitch; see the Step 1 illustration. Count up and over to begin stitching in the top left of that corner.

2 *Stitching:* Refer to the Cross-Stitch General Instructions and Stitches on page 158 and the Stitch Chart. Work cross-stitches using 2 strands of floss. Use 5 strands of Pale Geranium to work straight stitches on the clover flowers. Work back-stitches with 1 strand of Vy. Dk. Royal Blue.

3 *Pincushion:* Fold the stitched piece in half diagonally; see the Step 3A illustration. Stitch seam, leaving opening; turn right side out. Firmly stuff the triangle, then slipstitch the opening closed. See the Step 3B illustration to form a heart; sew the plastic ring to the back of the pincushion at the tacked points. Thread the wire-edge ribbon through the ring, and tie in a bow.

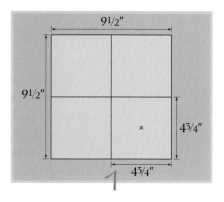

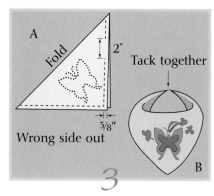

Butterfly Pincushion Color Key

Symbol	DMC #	Color	Symbol	DMC #	Color
■	30211	Lavender	▲	30800	Pale Delft
▲	30472	Ultra Avocado Green	x	33325	Baby
●	30553	Violet	—	30957	Pale Geranium Straight Stitches
=	30554	Violet			and Backstitches
●	30580	Moss Green	▬	30820	Royal Blue Backstitches
P	30581	Moss Green			

Hearts painted in spicy warm colors circle the lid of the large box, while individual hearts decorate the smaller ones inside. Tuck the mini boxes with assorted teas, potpourri, a "free lunch for two" coupon, coins, stamps or love notes to warm someone special's heart.

List of Materials

- Round papier mâché boxes: one 9½" (24.3 cm), seven 3" (7.5 cm)
- Acrylic paints: antique white, black, medium blue, clay, tumbleweed
- Paintbrushes: Nos. 2, 6, 12 flat; fine liner or spotter
- Black permanent-ink marker
- Pattern Sheet
- Miscellaneous items: pencil, ruler, tracing and graphite paper, stylus, paint palette, brush basin, paper towels

1 *Basecoat:* Refer to Painting Instructions and Techniques on page 160. Use 2 coats of paint, letting dry between coats. Basecoat entire lids and inside of small boxes antique white. Basecoat inside of large box clay. Basecoat outside of boxes blue. Use No. 12 flat brush to side-load tumbleweed on outer edge of lids to shade.

2 *Patterns:* Trace the pattern; use graphite paper and stylus to transfer entire pattern onto large box lid, and an individual heart onto small lids. Transfer outlines only on Hearts A and B, not any detail lines.

3 *Designs:* Use the liner brush to paint lettering clay. Basecoat Heart A blue and Heart B clay on both the large and small boxes; see the Step 3 illustration.

4 *Details:* Transfer details to A and B with graphite paper and stylus. Refer to the Heart Painting Guide and the photo to paint details on each heart.

5 *Finishing:* Use the liner brush and black paint or marking pen to outline lettering and hearts, as shown in the Step 5 illustration. Refer to the Box Lid Edge pattern and photo to paint or draw black mock stitches around edges of hearts and box lids.

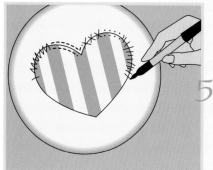

Box Lid Edge Pattern
2 of 2
(Pattern 1 is on Pattern Sheet)

Heart Painting Guide

A	Antique White Large Dots	E	Blue Stripes
B	Antique White Pinstripes	F	Clay Horizontal and Blue Vertical Lines
C	Blue "Stitch" Lines and Large Dots	G	Clay (1) and Blue (2) Pie Shapes
D	Clay Small Dots	H	Clay Mini-Checks

PARTY HEARTY
Piñata

This is a perfect centerpiece for a Valentine celebration; you can use it as a gift container, cardholder, or in the traditional way as a game filled with treats.

List of Materials

- 12″ to 15″ (30.5 to 38 cm) heart-shaped latex balloon

- 1 cup (250 mL) flour, or wheat wallpaper paste

- 3 yd. (2.75 m) each ribbon, ½″ (1.3 cm) wide: pink, dark pink, green, white

- Several sheets of tissue paper: pink, light pink

- 3 white ribbon roses with leaves, 3″ (7.5 cm)

- Glues: rubber cement, glue stick

- Miscellaneous items: newspapers, heavy-duty thread, ruler, paper towels, black marker, water, large bowl or pan, straight pin, scissors, masking tape

1 *Preparation:* Cover a flat work surface with several layers of newspaper. Tear, do not cut, newspaper sheets into 2" (5 cm) strips of varying lengths. Torn edges blend easier and add strength when covering the piñata.

2 *Balloon:* Inflate the ballon, and knot with thread. Place balloon on paper towels. See the Step 2 illustration and mark a 3" (7.5 cm) square on the back, 2" (5 cm) from the top, with black marker.

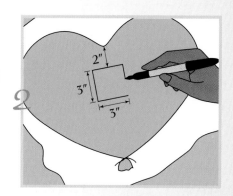

3 *Shell:* Mix a paste of 1 cup (250 mL) flour and 2 cups (500 mL) water very well in a large bowl. Dip newspaper strips in paste, 1 at a time. Blot any excess paste on paper towels, and cover the balloon with layers of paper strips. Alternate horizontal and vertical layers, completely covering the entire balloon, except the marked 3" (7.5 cm) square. Let dry; pop balloon with a pin. Remove balloon pieces, and trim edges of opening.

4 *Harness:* See the Step 4 illustration to wrap pink ribbon tightly around piñata edge, then around the center front and back, going from top to bottom. Ribbon should intersect at the center top and bottom. Tape with masking tape as needed to prevent slipping. Knot; tie ends to form a 6" (15 cm) loop hanger at the top.

5 *Fringing:* Fold each sheet of tissue paper crosswise, and cut into 3" (7.5 cm) strips; see the Step 5A illustration. Fold each strip in half lengthwise. Clip every ¼" (6 mm), to within ½" (1.3 cm) of cut edges to fringe; see 5B. You may fold and cut several sheets at once. Open each strip and refold lengthwise with opposite sides together; do not crease fold. Use glue stick to spot–glue straight edges together.

6 *Covering:* Place piñata in a large bowl or suspend it for easier covering; refer to the photo. Begin at the center front, and apply rubber cement in small areas at a time. Glue the straight edges of the fringed tissue strips; overlap to completely cover. Follow the heart shape as you glue, and alternate the pinks as shown. Fill piñata with treats before covering the opening.

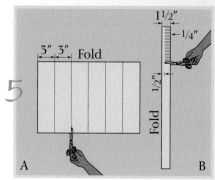

7 *Finishing:* Refer to the photo to glue the ribbon roses to the center front. Tie pink and white ribbons into multi-loop bows. Add several green ribbon streamers. Overlap and glue to bottom.

HOLIDAY
Bunnies

Dress up little muslin bunnies for Valentine's Day or the 4th of July. Once you see how easy it is, you could create a costumed bunny for every holiday!

List of Materials

For Both Bunnies

- 5" (12.5 cm) muslin bunny*
- Hot glue gun

For Valentine's Bunny

- Pink squeeze tip fabric paint
- 2" (5 cm) cutwork heart doily*
- Brass heart charm

- 1/4 yd. (0.25 m) red satin ribbon, 1/8" (3 mm) wide
- 1/4 yd. (0.25 m) red wire-edge ribbons, 5/8" (1.5 cm) and 2" (5 cm) wide

For 4th of July Bunny

- 1/8 yd. (0.15 m) red-and-white plaid 45" (115 cm) cotton fabric
- 4" (10 cm) Battenberg doily*

- 1/2" (1.3 cm) red ribbon rose
- 1/8 yd. (0.15 m) white tulle
- 1/3 yd. (0.32 m) red satin ribbon, 1/2" (1.3 cm) wide
- Miscellaneous items: ruler, scissors, sewing machine and matching threads, needle

*(See Sources on pg. 175 for purchasing information.)

34

Valentine's Bunny

1 *Preparation:* Paint I ♥ U in the center of the doily with the squeeze fabric paint. Tie ⅛″ (3 mm) ribbon through charm and tie in a bow around both ears.

2 *Skirt:* Pull wire on 1 edge of 2″ (5 cm) ribbon to gather. Fold under ½″ (1.3 cm) on 1 cut end. Tightly wrap ribbon around bunny's waist, overlapping ends ½″ (1.3 cm). See the Step 2 illustration to adjust gathers evenly and twist wires to secure. Hot-glue overlapped ends.

3 *Bodice/Sleeve:* Pull wire on 1 edge of ⅝″ (1.5 cm) ribbon to gather. Drape the ribbon around bunny's neck and shoulders. Tuck cut edges under center front waist of skirt and glue. Spot-glue ruffle to waist at center back, and skirt to waist. Hot-glue doily to hands.

4th of July Bunny

1 *Preparation:* Cut three 2″ x 15″ (5 x 38 cm) pieces from plaid fabric for dress. Sew pieces right sides together with ⅛″ (3 mm) seams.

2 *Dress:* Sew short ends of each dress piece together to make 3 tubes. Gather 1 tube along 1 long edge for skirt, and 2 tubes along both long edges for sleeves. Put skirt around bunny's waist; adjust gathers evenly. Knot to secure, and trim threads. Place the sleeves on bunny's arms; adjust gathers evenly at the shoulder. Knot to secure, and trim threads. Repeat to gather sleeve to fit around lower arm.

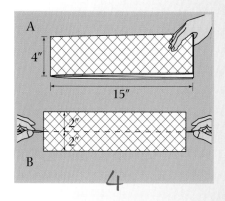

3 *Collar:* Cut a slit in the center of doily, and pull over bunny's head. Hot-glue to dress in back. Gather doily slightly under chin, and hot-glue to dress in front below chin. Hot-glue rose centered on doily front. Tie satin ribbon into a bow, and hot-glue to top of head.

4 *Slip:* Cut two 4″ x 30″ (10 x 76 cm) pieces of tulle. See the 4A illustration to fold each piece in half to make 4 thicknesses of tulle. Gather the tulle across the center as shown in 4B; pull the gathers to fit around the bunny's waist. Stitch together in back, slip onto bunny under dress, knot threads to secure, and trim ends.

Create this beautiful basket for St. Patrick's Day, and give it as a gift. Even if someone isn't Irish, getting blooming flowers and bright green plants in the middle of March will cause someone's eyes to be smiling

List of Materials

- Large green oval basket, 14" (35.5 cm) long, 6" (15 cm) deep and 12" (30.5 cm) high at handle
- Live plants: One 6" (15 cm) pot of peace lily or other upright green plant; one 6" (15 cm) pot of blooming white cyclamen, azalea or chrysanthemum; one 4"

- (10 cm) pot of variegated ivy; 1 or 2 other 4" (10 cm) pots; number needed depends on basket size
- 5 plastic saucers, 1 for each plant pot to sit in
- 3" x 4" x 8" (7.5 x 10 x 20.5 cm) brick dry floral foam
- 1 pkg. green sheet moss

- Greening pins, 24-gauge wire, floral pick
- 3 yd. (2.75 m) green sheer ribbon, 2" (5 cm) wide
- Three 12" (30.5 cm) shamrock picks
- Miscellaneous items: serrated knife, ruler, wire cutters

1 *Basket Preparation:* If you have been unable to find a green basket, you can easily make a natural-colored basket green. If the basket has wide reed pieces, such as shown in the photo, use a soft cloth to wipe green stain onto the basket. Wipe off any excess, and repeat until the basket is the desired shade. For wicker, or thicker twig baskets, spray paint will do the job. Follow manufacturer's instructions, and work in a well-ventilated area.

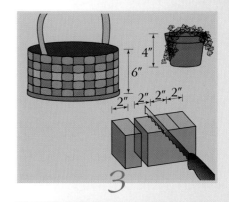

2 *Large Plants:* Place the 2 larger 6″ (15 cm) peace lily and cyclamen plants in the back of the basket. Place the lily on the left, and the cyclamen on the right. Place their plastic saucers underneath them.

3 *Foam Base:* Measure the inside depth of the basket. Measure the height of the 4″ (10 cm) diameter pots, usually about 4″ (10 cm). Subtract the pot height from the basket depth, and mark the floral foam brick on the top into slices that thick. See the Step 3 illustration to use the serrated knife to cut the floral foam brick into slices along the marked lines. Place 3 of the slices into the basket bottom in front of the 2 larger plants; these will provide a base for the smaller plants.

4 *Small Plants:* Place the plastic saucers on the foam slices, and the three 4″ (10 cm) plants into their saucers. Each plant should sit with the top of the plant pot level with the top of the basket; see the Step 4 illustration. If the plant pots are not fitting snugly into the basket, use additional plant to fill the space, or stuff in extra floral foam. Cover the entire basket surface with sheet moss. Pat down, and secure with 4-8 greening pins. The moss does not have to be very neat; let some spill out over the basket edges; as shown in the photo.

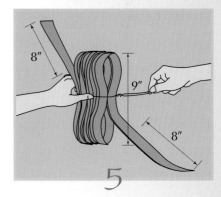

5 *Bow:* Make a 10-loop, 9″ (23 cm) bow with 8″ (20.5 cm) streamers, as shown in the Step 5 illustration. Twist 6″ (15 cm) of 24-gauge wire around bow; twist tightly. Wrap wire ends around a floral pick, and insert pick into foam at upper right side of basket. Stick the 3 shamrock picks into the foam around the cyclamen in the back right.

6 *Care:* Make sure to water each plant individually at least 2 times per week, even more often if the humidity is low.

LONG LEAN
Leprechaun

Who says all leprechauns are short, stout fellows with beards and pot bellies? Perhaps the long-legged ones are so fast that we never get to see them!

List of Materials

- ⅛ yd. (0.15 m) each cotton fabrics: unbleached muslin, green/white stripe, green/gold star print, green/brown print, solid green
- Polyester fiberfill
- Fabric paints or permanent–ink markers: black, white, green
- Fine-liner paintbrush
- ¼ yd. (0.25 m) each ribbon: 1½" (3.8 cm) plaid satin, ¼" (6 mm) gold satin, ⅝" (1.5 cm) decorative woven
- ¾" (2 cm) round decorative gold shank button
- Red mohair doll hair
- 2" (5 cm) acorn cap or other mini hat
- Pattern Sheet
- Miscellaneous items: tracing paper, pencil, scissors, sewing machine and matching threads, iron, straight pins, chopstick or knitting needle, sewing needle, cotton swab, powdered blush, white craft glue

St. Patrick's Day   St. Patrick's Day   St. Patrick's Day   St. Patrick's Day

1 *Preparation:* Trace the 8 patterns onto tracing paper with pencil; cut out. Cut out the pattern pieces from the fabrics as indicated. Stitch all fabrics right sides together with 1/4″ (6 mm) seams, unless otherwise indicated. Clip curves and corners; trim seams.

2 *Shoes, Stockings, Trousers, & Shirt:* Follow the Step 2 illustration to stitch a shoe to a stocking, a stocking to a trouser bottom, and a trouser waist to a shirt bottom. Press all seams open; you should now have 2 long body pieces.

3 *Body:* Pin the body pieces together, matching at the 3 seams. Start at the neck and stitch all the way down, and around back up to the neck, as shown in the Step 2 illustration. Make sure to leave the neck unstitched, as well as the opening on 1 side. Turn the body right side out. Stuff firmly with fiberfill, using chopstick to reach way down into the shoes. Slipstitch opening closed.

4 *Face:* Place 1 head piece over the pattern piece, and trace the face details with pencil. Use the liner brush and black fabric paint, or marker, to make the eyebrows, mouth, nose and chin. Outline the eyes and color the pupil with black. Color the rest of the eye green, and dot the pupil with white. Let dry; use cotton swab to brush the cheeks with blush.

5 *Head:* Stitch head pieces together, leaving neck open. Turn right side out; stuff firmly with fiberfill. Turn the shirt neck edge under 1/4″

(6 mm). See the Step 5 illustration to insert the neck 1/2″ (1.3 cm) into the shirt neck opening, and slipstitch head to the neck.

6 *Ear:* Stitch 2 ear pieces together. Refer to the pattern to cut a slit through the ear back, cutting through 1 layer of fabric only. Turn ear right side out through the slit. Topstitch around the ear 1/8″ (3 mm) from the edge.

7 *Arm:* Stitch a hand piece to the bottom of each sleeve; press seams open. Stitch sleeve/hand pieces together, leaving open on sleeve where indicated on pattern. Turn right side out, stuff firmly with fiberfill, and slipstitch opening closed. Refer to the photo to tack arm to body at shoulder, making sure thumbs point in.

8 *Bow Tie:* Cut 6″ (15 cm) of plaid ribbon. See the Step 8A illustration to fold the ribbon to the center, overlapping the ends in back. Baste through all layers, and pull the thread ends to gather. Knot, and trim thread ends. Pleat the remaining ribbon piece to a 3/8″ (1 cm) width; see 8B. Tightly wrap around gathers on bow, tack ends together in back. Use craft glue and glue bow under chin.

9 *Finishing:* Glue gold satin ribbon around waist, overlapping ends in front. Remove shank from button, and glue over ribbon ends. Cut woven ribbon in half; wrap each piece around ankle. Overlap ends at inner ankles, and glue. Glue ears to side of head, with slit to the inside. Glue doll hair to head, and cap over hair.

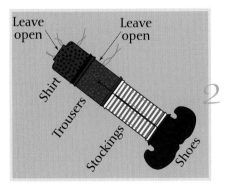

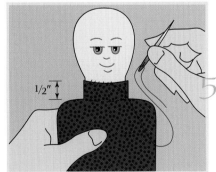

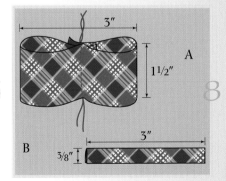

SHIMMERING
Shamrock Shirt

You'll be wearing o' the green for sure with this shirt! It's decorated with shamrocks made of freezer paper that are ironed to the shirt and covered with metallic and pearl fabric paints. After the paper patterns are removed, it looks like a shower of shamrocks shimmering on the shirt.

List of Materials

- Gray or white sweatshirt or T-shirt
- T-shirt board or cardboard
- Freezer paper
- Fabric paints: metallic silver and pearls: lime green, teal, green
- 1" (2.5 cm) sponge brush

- Palette knife
- Metallic silver fine-line fabric marker
- Pattern Page 167
- Miscellaneous items: iron, masking tape, tracing paper, pencil, scissors, paint palette, paper towels

1 *Preparation:* Wash and dry sweatshirt as you will after wearing; do not use fabric softener. Turn shirt inside out and iron freezer or wax paper to inside front of shirt, shiny side toward shirt. Place the paper widths side by side, cutting them to fit where necessary. Turn shirt right side out. Cover the entire area on the inside front where the design will go; this will prevent the paint from seeping through. Insert T-shirt board or cardboard into shirt. Tape shirt on back side of cardboard with masking tape to make a wrinkle-free surface on the front.

2 *Patterns:* Trace 3 shamrock patterns to tracing paper with pencil, and cut out. Place the shamrock patterns on freezer paper and trace around them as directed on patterns; cut out. Refer to the photo and the Step 2 illustration to arrange 11 shamrocks on shirt, shiny side toward shirt. Iron shamrocks onto sweatshirt.

3 *Painting:* Squeeze a blob of each of the 4 paints, the size of a fifty-cent piece, onto the paint palette. Referring to the photo, quickly apply a wavy line of each of the 4 colors of fabric paint over the paper shamrocks with the 1″ (2.5 cm) sponge brush. Do the greens light to darker and the metallic silver last.

4 *Blending:* Quickly drag the palette knife diagonally across the paint to blend, as shown in the Step 4 illustration. Wipe excess paint on paper towel. Repeat until all paint has been blended; but do not overblend. Remove paper shamrocks; let dry flat.

5 *Finishing:* See the Step 5 illustration to outline the shamrocks with silver marker. Heat-set paints following manufacturer's instructions. Remove the masking tape, T-shirt board or cardboard and freezer paper from the inside front of the shirt. Launder following fabric paint manufacturer's instructions.

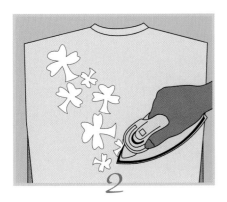

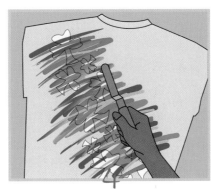

The Hebrew symbols for "Passover" are stitched in shades of salmon and bordered in royal blue on a premade placemat and napkin. For non-Jewish stitchers, create your family heirloom with cross-stitched Easter lilies in shades of yellow, white and green accented with a soft blue banner proclaiming "He is risen!"

List of Materials

For One Placemat & Napkin

- 14-count ecru prefinished evenweave 13" x 18" (33 x 46 cm) placemat and 15" (38 cm) square napkin*—measurements include fringe

- 1 skein each 6-strand DMC embroidery floss in colors listed on the Color Keys

- Metallic light gold thread (282Z) (for Passover table setting only)

- No. 24 tapestry needle

- Stitch Charts on pages 44 and 45

- Miscellaneous items: scissors, 2 terrycloth towels, iron

*(See Sources on pg. 175 for purchasing information.)

1 *Preparation:* Refer to the Cross-Stitch General Instructions and Stitches on page 158 and the Stitch Charts on pages 44 and 45. Cross-stitch the designs using 2 strands of floss. Each square on the graphs represents 1 square of cloth. Symbols correspond to colors in the Color Key.

2 *Passover Setting:* Count 5 threads up and over from lower left corner of the placemat and napkin to begin stitching the lower leftmost point of the design. Refer to the photo to continue cross-stitching border around entire placemat. Use a single strand of metallic gold to backstitch around the letters.

3 *Easter Setting:* Count 12 threads up and 7 threads over from lower left corner to begin stitching on the placemat at the leftmost lower edge of the banner. Refer to the photo to continue cross-stitching border around entire placemat. Count 7 threads up and 8 threads over from lower left corner of napkin to begin stitching at the base of the lily stem. Use 2 strands of Vy. Dk. Mocha No. 3031 to backstitch "He is risen!" on the banner and 1 strand for all other backstitches.

Continued

Passover Placemat Stitch Chart

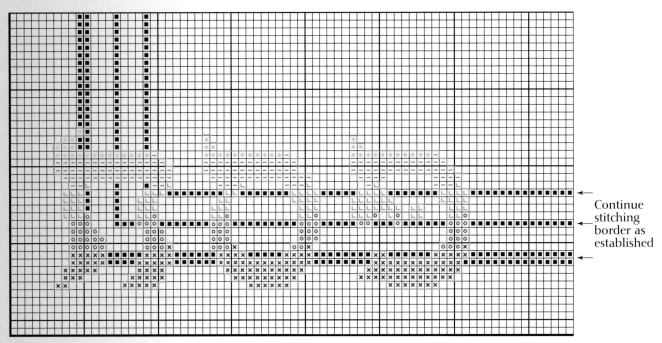

← Continue stitching border as established

Passover Napkin Stitch Chart

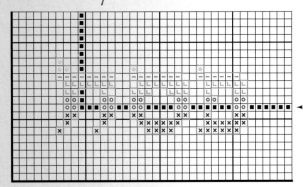

← Continue stitching border as established

Passover Setting Color Key

Symbol	DMC #	Color
×	347	Vy. Dk. Salmon
–	760	Salmon
·	761	Lt. Salmon
■	797	Royal Blue
○	3328	Dk. Salmon
L	3712	Med. Salmon
–	282Z	Metallic Gold Backstitches

Easter Placemat Stitch Chart

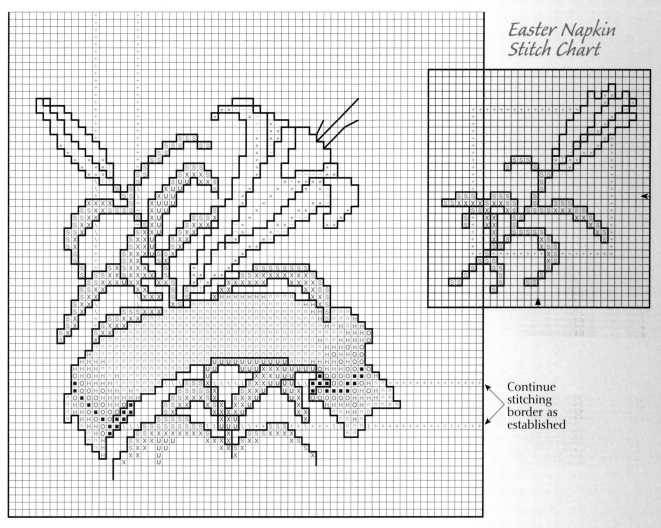

Easter Napkin Stitch Chart

Continue stitching border as established

Easter Setting Color Key

Symbol	DMC #	Color	Symbol	DMC #	Color
X	320	Med. Pistachio Green	■	826	Med. Blue
U	367	Dk. Pistachio Green	H	827	Vy. Lt. Blue
S	368	Lt. Pistachio Green	n	828	Ultra Vy. Lt. Blue
T	369	Vy. Lt. Pistachio Green	+	963	Ultra Vy. Lt. Dusty Rose
-	677	Vy. Lt. Old Gold	\	3716	Vy. Lt. Dusty Rose
•	746	Off White	—	3031	Vy. Dk. Mocha Backstitches (1 strand)
O	813	Lt. Blue	—	3031	Vy. Dk. Mocha Backstitches (2 strands)

Here's an Easter basket for someone a little older, who might not be waiting for candy from the Big Bunny. Fresh flowers and greens bring a breath of springtime air into a shut-in's or dear friend's home, in addition to saying "Happy Easter!"

List of Materials

- Large rectangular natural basket, 7" x 10" (18 x 25.5 cm), 6" (15 cm) deep, and 12" (30.5 cm) high at handle
- Plastic liner for basket, available from your local florist or craft store
- 2 bricks 3" x 4" x 8" (7.5 x 10 x 20.5 cm) wet arrangement floral foam

- Live florals, available from your local florist or craft store: 4 myrtle branches, about 30" (76 cm) tall; 3 purple iris; 5 pink tulips; 1 branch each of yellow daisies and purple spray asters
- Green floral tape, greening pins
- 1 pkg. green sheet moss

- 2 yd. (1.85 m) purple gingham ribbon, 2" (5 cm) wide
- Small stuffed duck
- Miscellaneous items: serrated knife, ruler, scissors, sharp knife, cutting board or surface, rubber band, plastic wrap or artificial Easter grass

1 *Preparation:* Soak floral foam in the sink for at least 30 minutes. Place the plastic basket liner into the basket. Use serrated knife to trim the foam bricks so they fit securely into the basket liner. The top of the foam should be ½" (1.3 cm) above the basket and liner top.

2 *Foam Base:* Place floral tape diagonally across the bricks, to hold them together. See the Step 2 illustration. Fill the basket liner with water. Cover the entire basket surface with sheet moss. Pat down, and secure with 4-8 greening pins. The moss does not have to be very neat; let some spill out over the basket edges, as shown in the photo.

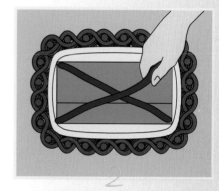

3 *Myrtle Branches:* Use a sharp knife on a cutting surface to cut off the bottom 2" to 3" (5 to 7.5 cm) from the myrtle branch stems, 1 at a time. Remove any leaves from the bottom 6" (15 cm) that will go into the floral foam. Place the 4 branches as shown in the Step 3A illustration, pushing them straight down into the foam. Pull the branches together at the top; hold them together with a rubber band. Tie the purple gingham ribbon around the rubber band and make a bow, as shown in 3B.

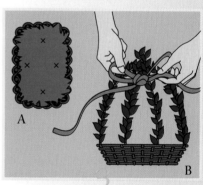

A

B

4 *Iris, Asters, Daisies and Tulips:* Snap off the daisies and the asters from their branches with your fingers. Use a sharp knife on a cutting surface to cut the individual flower stems, 1 at a time, to varying heights. Remove any leaves from the bottom that will go into the floral foam. Refer to the photo; the tallest iris is about 9" (23 cm), the tulips are about 6" to 8" (15 to 20.5 cm). Group the flowers in corners of the basket as shown in the Step 4 illustration and the photo.

5 *Stuffed Animal:* Place a small piece of plastic wrap or artificial Easter grass in the basket center; place the stuffed duck on the plastic. Remove the animal when watering the basket each day. Remove the flowers as they wilt, until all you have left are the branches, or replace the flowers with fresh ones as needed. The myrtle branches can last up to 1 month with proper care.

Daisies

Iris

Spray Aster

Tulips

CHURCH IN
the Valley

The whole family can join in the fun of getting this birdhouse converted to a church in time for Easter Sunday service in Spring Valley. The congregation is ready and waiting!

List of Materials

- 6.5" x 7" x 8.5" (16.3 x 18 x 21.8 cm) wooden birdhouse*
- 8" x 4" (20.5 x 10 cm) wood, 1" (2.5 cm) thick
- Jigsaw or scroll saw
- Gesso
- Acrylic craft paints: white, light blue, olive green, pink

- Paintbrushes: No. 10 flat, 1" (2.5 cm) sponge
- ½" (1.3 cm) masking tape
- Small cup hook
- 1" (2.5 cm) liberty bell
- 1 sheet shrink plastic
- Permanent markers: red, blue, yellow, green, black extra-fine

- Pattern Page 163
- Miscellaneous items: tracing and graphite paper, pencil, sandpaper, tack cloth, paint palette, sponge, ruler, scissors, white craft glue, needlenose pliers

*(See Sources on pg. 175 for purchasing information.)

1 *Steeple:* Refer to Painting Instructions and Techniques on page 160. Trace steeple pattern to tracing paper, and cut out; transfer to wood. Cut out from wood with jigsaw or scroll saw. Sand birdhouse and steeple; remove sanding dust with tack cloth.

2 *Sponging:* Use sponge brush to basecoat church and steeple with 2 coats of gesso; let dry. Basecoat church and steeple with white paint, and church base with olive green. Let dry. Pour some light blue paint on palette. Use small damp sponge to lightly sponge-paint front, back and sides of church and steeple.

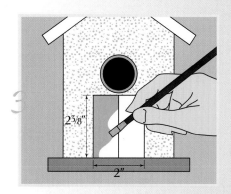

3 *Doors:* Draw doors 2″ (5 cm) wide by 2⅜″ (6.2 cm) high on center front of church with ruler and pencil; refer to the Step 3 illustration. Use the No. 10 flat brush to paint inside edge of birdhouse hole, doors and perch pink; let dry. Outline and draw center line with ruler and black marker.

4 *Roof:* Apply strips of masking tape side by side across the top of the birdhouse roof. Remove every other strip, and use a credit card or hard plastic surface to rub down the tape edges well. See the Step 4 illustration to use sponge brush to paint the roof stripes and all roof edges pink. Let dry; remove masking tape.

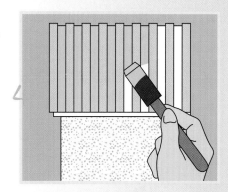

5 *Windows:* Place shrink plastic over the window pattern, and trace 10 windows using black marker and ruler. Color the windows with the red, green, blue and yellow markers, being careful not to run into or smear the black marker lines. Retrace any black lines, if necessary. Let markers dry for at least 1 hour. Cut out windows with scissors.

6 *Gluing Windows:* Lightly mark church with pencil for window placement. Refer to photo and Step 6 illustration to place bottom of windows 1″ (2.5 cm) up from church base–3 windows on each side and 2 each on the front and back. Apply white craft glue to the colored side of the windows, and glue to the church.

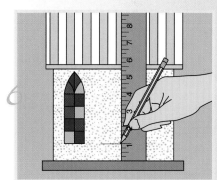

7 *Finishing:* Screw cup hook into center of steeple peak 1″ (2.5 cm) from the tip. Slip bell onto hook, and close hook with needle-nose pliers. Glue steeple onto the roof with the front of the steeple 2″ (5 cm) from the front of the church roof. Place a small amount of glue on the perch and insert into the hole.

*S*end a note to "somebunny" special on Corrugated Easter Cards you made yourself. They're perfect for an invitation to your Easter egg hunt or sunrise breakfast.

List of Materials

- 2 sheets 8½" x 11" (21.8 x 28 cm) parchment cardstock (enough for 4 cards)
- Scraps of pastel cotton fabrics: lavender, blue, green
- 4" x 12" (10 x 30.5 cm) corrugated cardboard

- ⅜ yd. (0.35 m) paper-backed fusible web
- Acrylic paints: brown, dark brown, white, pink, turquoise, lavender, gray
- Paintbrushes: 5 stencil; 1" (2.5 cm) sponge

- Black fine-line permanent-ink marker
- Pattern Page 164
- Miscellaneous items: scissors, ruler, iron, pencil, tracing paper, paper towels, paint palette, white paper

1 *Preparation:* Cut parchment sheets in half, measuring 8½" x 5½" (21.8 x 14 cm). Fold in half again to make 4½" x 5½" (11.5 x 14 cm) cards. Take 4" x 12" (10 x 30.5 cm) piece of corrugated cardboard. Peel off 1 layer of the cardboard to reveal the corrugation.

2 *Patterns:* Follow manufacturer's instructions to fuse paper-backed web to wrong side of fabrics and cardboard; cut out. Trace the 3 patterns to tracing paper, and cut out. Find appropriate fabric scraps to fit pattern pieces, and cut out.

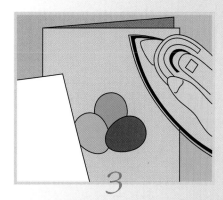

3

3 *Fusing Fabric:* Refer to photo to position the following fabric pieces on card fronts: green, blue, then lavender eggs on Basket Card; green top and lavender bottom on Egg Card; and blue egg on Bunny Card. Fuse fabric to cards, placing a sheet of white paper between the iron and the card; see the Step 3 illustration.

4 *Basecoating Cardboard:* Refer to Painting Instructions and Techniques on page 160. Basecoat cardboard pieces on the corrugated front side with 2 coats of paint and sponge brush, letting dry between coats. Be sure to get paint in all crevices and on the outer edges of cardboard. Paint as follows: Egg Card center, turquoise; Bunny Card bunny, white; and nose, pink; Basket Card basket, brown.

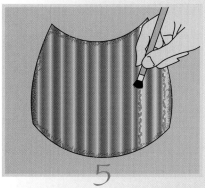

5

5 *Dry-Brushing Cardboard:* See the Step 5 illustration and refer to the following to dry-brush the cardboard pieces with the 5 stencil brushes:

Egg Card Egg	Outer Edges Stripes	Lavender Pink and White
Bunny Card Bunny	Ears & Cheeks Outer Edges	Pink Gray
Basket Card Basket	Outer Edges	Dark Brown

6 *Fusing Cardboard:* Refer to Step 3 to fuse cardboard pieces over fabric pieces on the cards. Lightly iron from the inside of the card also, to better adhere the cardboard. Make eyes, nose, mouth and cheek dots on Bunny Card with permanent marker; see the Step 6 illustration.

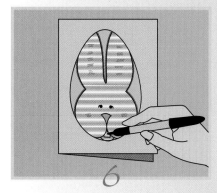

6

EASY
Easter Appliqué

The magic of fusible web bonds fabrics together and makes quick work of the "appliquéd" egg basket and bunnies on a wall hanging and matching premade pillow. So hop to it and heat up your iron to make these quick quilt designs.

List of Materials

- 45" (115 cm) cotton fabrics: ½ yd. (0.5 m) each aqua print and dark blue print; ⅛ yd. (0.15 m) each white, blue, pale yellow, rose tone-on-tone prints; ⅝ yd. (0.6 m) coordinating print

- 13 yd. (11.96 m) rose print fabric ribbon, ⅞" (2.2 cm) wide

- Paper-backed fusible web: 13 yd. (11.96 m) tape, ⅞" (2.2 cm) wide; ½ yd. (0.5 m) sheet, 17" (45 cm) wide

- 7 yd. (6.4 m) rose craft yarn

- 7 white pom-poms, ½" (1.3 cm) diameter

- Quilt batting

- 14" (35.5 cm) square premade muslin pillow cover and pillow form

- Fabric glue

- Pattern Sheet

- Miscellaneous items: tracing paper, pencil, scissors, yardstick, iron, disappearing-ink pen, straight pins, safety pins, darning needle

Rose Print Fabric Ribbon

Length	# to Cut	Use	Length	# to Cut	Use
28½" (72.3 cm)	4	Quilt border/binding	12" (30.5 cm)	4	Pillow border
20½" (52.3 cm)	4	Quilt border/binding	11" (28 cm)	2	Pillow background lattice
17½" (44.3 cm)	4	Quilt background lattice	7½" (19.3 cm)	1	Pillow basket top
6⅜" (16 cm)	8	Quilt background lattice	4½" (11.5 cm)	2	Pillow basket
16" (40.5 cm)	1	Quilt basket top	2½" (6.5 cm)	2	Pillow basket
9½" (24.3 cm)	2	Quilt basket			
7" (18 cm)	2	Quilt basket			
5" (12.5 cm)	2	Quilt basket			
2½" (6.5 cm)	2	Quilt basket			

Fabric

Size	# to Cut	Use	Fabric
4½" x 17" (11.5 x 43 cm)	2	White bunnies	Sheet fusible web
4½" x 8" (11.5 x 20.5 cm)	3	Eggs	Sheet fusible web
2¼" x 45" (6 x 115 cm)	3	Dark blue print	Borders
16" x 24" (40.5 x 61 cm)	1	Aqua print	Quilt background
11" (28 cm) square	1	Aqua print	Pillow background
20½" x 28½" (52.3 x 72.3 cm)	1 each	Quilt layers	Backing fabric and batting

1 *Preparation:* Fuse ⅞" (2.2 cm) fusible tape to rose ribbon. **Do not remove paper backing.** See the Cutting Guide to cut rose ribbon lengths and fabrics. On 2 of the 28½" (72.3 cm) ribbon lengths, mark 2¼" (6 cm) from each end. Carefully slice through paper backing; do not cut ribbon. See the Step 1 illustration to remove paper backing between cuts; **do not remove paper at ends,** but remove paper backing on all other fused ribbon.

2 *Bunny & Eggs:* Trace the 4 patterns to tracing paper, and cut out. Fuse 17" (43 cm) fusible web lengths side by side to wrong side of white fabric and 8" (20.5 cm) lengths to wrong side of yellow, blue and rose fabrics. Cut bunny and eggs as indicated on patterns from fused fabrics; remove paper backing.

3 *Quilt Baskets:* Place quilt background fabric, right side up, on flat work surface that can withstand heat of iron. See the Step 3A illustration and mark as shown with disappearing-ink pen. Use pattern to cut 1 each quilt and pillow basket from remaining blue print. Place quilt basket, right side up, on work surface. See the Step 3B illustration to weave the ribbons 1⅜" (3.5 cm) apart on the basket, and pin. Trim ribbon ends flush with basket edge; fuse.

Continued

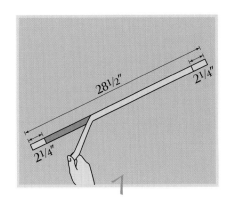

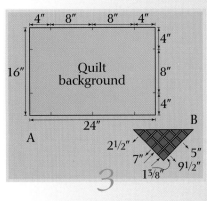

4   *Background Lattice:* See Step 4 illustration to place the 6³⁄₈" (16 cm) ribbons on the background. Use the yardstick to line up and measure ribbons. Pin, trim ribbon ends, and fuse.

5   *Basket Assembly:* See the Step 5 illustration to place the center bunny, eggs and basket on quilt, all overlapping. Place the 17¹⁄₂" (44.3 cm) ribbons overlapping basket edges to make sure ribbons don't cover eggs and bunny. Remove ribbons and fuse bunny, eggs and basket. Fuse the 16" (40.5 cm) ribbon along the basket top, and the remaining 4 lattice ribbons; trim ribbon ends. Center 4 other bunnies in diamonds, and fuse; glue on pom-pom tails.

6   *Borders:* Cut 1 border strip in half, and trim each to 2¹⁄₄" x 21" (6 x 53.5 cm). Trim remaining strips to 24" (61 cm), and place at quilt top and bottom, abutting but not overlapping edges. Center the 28¹⁄₂" (72.3 cm) ribbons with paper backing over each "seam," and fuse; remove paper. Place remaining borders at each side; place the unfused ends of horizontal ribbons over side borders, and fuse. Center the 20¹⁄₂" (52.3 cm) ribbons over "seams," and fuse, crisscrossing ribbons. Trim excess borders to square off corners.

7   *Quilting:* Layer backing facedown, batting and quilt top faceup. Baste with safety pins every 5" (12.5 cm). Cut 15 pieces 12" (30.5 cm) long from pink yarn; thread darning needle with 1. Refer to the photo for placement, and insert needle front to back through all layers, then back to front, taking a small stitch. Separate the yarn strands to frizz; tie ends in a bow. Repeat for all bows.

8   *Binding:* Fold two 28¹⁄₂" (72.3 cm) ribbons in half lengthwise; place over top and bottom edges to encase. Fuse 1 at a time, molding with fingers while ribbon cools. Repeat to bind side edges.

9   *Pillow Preparation:* Press pillow cover. See the Step 9 illustration to mark centers on the 11" (28 cm) aqua square and weave ribbons 1" (2.5 cm) apart on pillow basket. Trim ribbon ends flush, and fuse marked aqua square on pillow cover front.

10   *Pillow Assembly:* Refer to the Step 10 illustration; place basket between marks in 1 corner, tuck under the eggs, remove the basket, and fuse eggs. Fuse the basket, basket top and lattice ribbons. Fuse the aqua square to the pillow cover front with the border ribbons. Center the bunnies in the squares, fuse, and glue on pom-poms. Cut five 12" (30.5 cm) lengths of yarn; separate strands to frizz. Tie each in a bow. Refer to the photo to glue bows to bunnies, basket and pillow center. Insert pillow form.

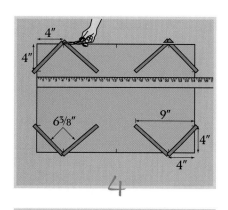

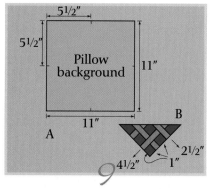

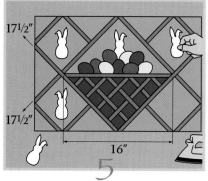

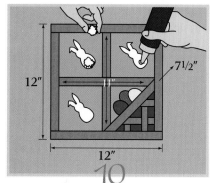

Shells saved from dyed eggs decorate an Eggshell Box to hold stickers, rubber stamps or even treats from the Easter Bunny.

List of Materials

- Chipwood or papier mâché oval box
- Dyed eggshells
- Paints: white metallic acrylic, iridescent brush-on glitter
- Medium flat paint or sponge brush
- White craft glue
- Gloss acrylic spray finish
- Miscellaneous items: paint palette, newspapers

1 *Basecoating:* Paint entire box and lid, inside and out, with 2 coats of white metallic paint.

2 *Decorating:* Break eggshells into small pieces. Brush glue onto lid top, lid sides and box sides, working in 1 area at a time; see the Step 2 illustration. Do not apply glue to the area on the box sides where lid overlaps. Refer to the photo to place eggshells, dyed side up, in glue.

3 *Finishing:* Brush iridescent glitter paint over entire box and lid. Lightly spray box and lid with 1 coat of finish, following manufacturer's instructions.

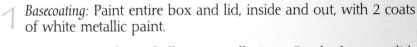

Here's a clever way to get double-duty out of table placemats. Use our patterns and instructions to make the jack-o'-lantern and Easter egg design, or create your own for your favorite holidays.

List of Materials

For Each Placemat

- 12" x 18" (30.5 x 46 cm) artist's canvas placemat
- Gesso
- Acrylic craft paints: brown, white, yellow, orange, light green, light pink, light blue
- Paintbrushes: 1" (2.5 cm) sponge, No. 4 and No. 8 flat, liner

- Water-base varnish
- Pattern Sheet
- Miscellaneous items: tracing and graphite paper, pencil, scissors, paint palette

1 *Preparation and Patterns:* Refer to the photo and illustrations for all Steps below. Refer to the Painting Instructions and Techniques on page 160. Let paint dry between colors and coats. Use the 1" (2.5 cm) sponge brush and gesso to prime any uncoated sides of the placemat. Trace 4 pumpkin face patterns to tracing paper; cut out. Place pumpkin patterns on placemat; trace lightly around them with pencil.

2 *Painting Pumpkin:* Use the No. 4 flat brush to paint the stem brown, and the eyes, nose and mouth yellow. Use the sponge brush to basecoat the pumpkin orange. Use graphite paper to transfer the eye, nose and mouth detail, or draw them in freehand.

3 *Pumpkin Details:* Shade around the eyes, nose and mouth with liner brush and brown paint, in the areas indicated by number on the pattern—1 means a light shade, and 2 a darker shade; see the Step 3 illustration. Use liner brush to make angle lines at the corners. Use the No. 4 brush to highlight lines around stem and pumpkin grooves with white/yellow mix. Shade the stem and around it, and the lower pumpkin with black/brown mix.

4 *Easter Egg Design:* Follow the Step 4 illustration to sketch design lines on the opposite side of the placemat. Begin in the center for all lines, and work out to the sides. Draw the thin green line

9½" (24.3 cm) from the top; curve both ends up about 1" (2.5 cm) higher than the center. All other lines should follow that curve; but make it more pronounced at the egg top and bottom.

5 *Painting Easter Egg:* Use the No. 4 brush to paint with blue the double lines and the wide curvy line near the bottom. Add a little white to make light blue, and paint the egg top, and between and below the double blue lines. Add a little white to green to make light green, and paint the area above and below the zigzag line with the No. 8 brush. Use the No. 8 brush to paint with pink the area below the middle line, the bottom and the 4 large dots; see the Step 5 illustration.

6 *Easter Egg Details:* Paint the following yellow: zigzag line at the top and the curvy line at the bottom with No. 8 brush, the top thin line with liner brush, scallops over the pink with the No. 4 brush. Use the No. 4 brush to paint with green the middle line and the curvy thin line near the bottom. Use the liner brush handle to make blue dots between the double blue lines.

7 *Finishing:* Use the liner brush to touch up any messy areas. Follow the manufacturer's instructions to apply 3 coats of varnish with sponge brush to each side of the placemat. Wipe off with a damp cloth after each use. Make sure they are completely dry before storing them flat.

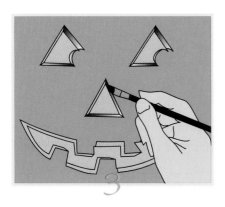

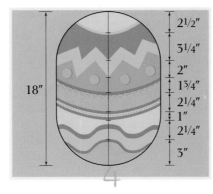

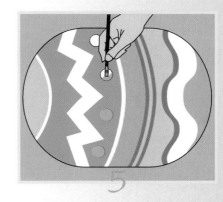

57

CLAY
Jointed Bunny

An air-dry clay bunny, strung on satin ribbon and joined with wire, is a lovely non-candy gift for the Easter basket, best friend or the kids' teachers.

List of Materials

- 6 oz. (175 g) white air-dry modeling clay
- Acrylic craft paints: magenta, purple, black, green, orange
- Paintbrushes: No. 2 round, No. 8 flat
- Glossy acrylic sealer
- 1 yd. (0.95 m) white satin ribbon, 1/4" (6 mm) wide
- 7 1/2" (19.3 cm) 24-gauge wire
- Pattern Page 165
- Miscellaneous items: tracing paper, pencil, wax paper, rolling pin, craft knife, drinking straw, paper towels, emery board, soft cloth, paint palette, black extra-fine-point permanent-ink marker, wire cutters, needlenose pliers

1 *Clay:* Trace 6 pattern pieces to tracing paper; cut out. Place clay on wax paper on hard work surface. Use rolling pin to flatten to 1/4" (6 mm) thickness. Place patterns on clay; use pencil to trace around the outlines; remove pattern.

2 *Cutting:* Use the craft knife to cut out clay and straw to punch holes in clay where shown on patterns and in the illustration. Carefully lift shapes, and use fingers to smooth edges. Let dry on paper towel, turning occasionally. When dry, smooth rough edges with emery board. Remove dust with soft cloth.

3 *Painting:* Refer to pattern and photo to use No. 2 brush and magenta to paint nose, bellybutton and toes. Thin magenta with water, and blush cheeks. Use No. 8 brush to paint bow purple, carrot orange, and carrot top green. Let paint dry; draw in detail lines and heart eyes with black marker.

4 *Finishing:* Use No. 8 brush to apply sealer to each piece on all sides; let dry. Thread ribbon through top hole; make an overhand knot for hanger. Cut wire into 5 pieces. Put wire in holes from front side, twist wire ends

to back, to wire pieces together loosely. For children, attach body pieces with ribbon instead of wire.

*J*t only looks like hand-painted porcelain; it could be a ceramic, greenware or papier mâché bunny decoupaged with floral prints from paper napkins.

List of Materials

- Bunny: papier mâché, greenware, ceramic
- Acrylic craft paints: white, metallic gold
- Paintbrushes: No. 10 flat, No. 1 liner
- White floral paper napkins
- Decoupage glue/sealer
- Acrylic spray finish

1 Preparation: Basecoat bunny on top and base with white paint and No. 10 brush. Use the liner brush to paint the eyes metallic gold. Apply 1 or 2 coats for complete coverage; let dry between all painting and gluing coats.

2 Floral Designs: Napkins are sometimes made of paper layers; only use the top printed layer. Tear desired floral designs from napkins; torn edges are less noticeable when decoupaged. Lay out floral designs on bunny until you have enough to cover the top of the bunny.

3 Decoupaging: Use flat brush to apply glue/sealer on a small area of the bunny body. Place the floral design on the glue, and carefully press down. Pat the design with the brush, then smooth with your fingers to remove air bubbles or wrinkles. Work from the center outward. If floral design tears or wrinkles don't come out, wash off the bunny and apply a new design. Let dry, then apply another coat of glue over each design.

4 Finishing: Repeat to decorate the entire bunny, overlapping napkin floral design edges to completely cover; see the illustration. When glue is completely dry, spray bunny with several coats of acrylic finish, following manufacturer's instructions.

NAPPLIQUÉ
Bunny Shirt

Here's an easy no-sew appliqué technique using paper napkins. Their interesting finish came from the moiré design on the napkins, but pastel or print napkins would work equally well.

List of Materials

- Good-quality paper napkins: light and dark mauve, burgundy, peach
- Water-soluble disappearing marker
- T-shirt
- T-shirt board or cardboard
- Fabric glue
- 1" (2.5 cm) sponge brush
- Blue-green fabric paints
- Palette knife
- Pattern Page 165
- Miscellaneous items: tracing paper, pencil, scissors, masking tape, wax paper, rolling pin, paint palette, press cloth, iron

1 *Preparation:* Wash and dry T-shirt as you will after wearing; do not use fabric softener. Trace bunny pattern to tracing paper; cut out. Trace 2 bunnies onto napkin with disappearing marker. Reverse pattern, and trace 2 more.

2 *Bunnies:* Napkins are sometimes made of layers of paper; only use 1 layer. Cut a rough square around each bunny, leaving about 2″ (5 cm) of napkin all around. See the Step 2 illustration to gently begin to tear out each bunny from a napkin, working in small sections at a time. Do not cut out with scissors; tearing gives bunnies a furry look.

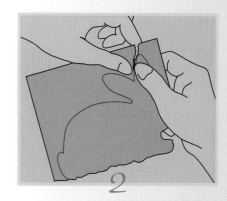

3 *Placement:* Insert T-shirt board or cardboard into T-shirt. Tape shirt on back side with masking tape to make a smooth surface on the front. Refer to photo to arrange napkin bunnies on T-shirt. Trace around each bunny onto shirt with disappearing marker. Remove bunnies from shirt.

4 *Gluing:* Use sponge brush to apply a generous amount of fabric glue inside and right up to the marker outline for 1 bunny. Place napkin bunny over the glue, and quickly press down as shown in the Step 4 illustration. Work from the center outward. You may choose to place a piece of wax paper over the bunny, and roll it flat with a rolling pin. Small wrinkles will smooth out as napkin dries. If there are large wrinkles, peel off the bunny and tear out a new one. Repeat to glue all 4 bunnies. Apply another layer of fabric glue over bunnies, being careful to get all around the edges to seal. Let dry.

5 *Painting Grass:* Apply an uneven line of blue-green fabric paint at the bottom of each bunny for grass. See the Step 5 illustration to use palette knife to pull paint up onto bunny and below on shirt to resemble blades of grass.

6 *Heat Setting/Care:* Cover bunnies with a dry press cloth. Use a dry iron on medium for 10 seconds on each side. Let glue dry several days before washing. Wash in cool water and line dry; do not dry-clean.

HIP-HOP-TOE
Game

Sure to appeal to the little kid in all of us is the game of Hip-Hop-Toe. If you line up three miniature eggs or bunnies in a row on the egg-shaped game board, you'll be the winner!

List of Materials

- 3½" x 5" (9 x 12.5 cm) unfinished oval wood plaque with routed edge
- Eight ¾" (2 cm) wood eggs
- ½ yd. (0.5 m) green satin ribbon, ⅛" (3 mm) wide
- 2" (5 cm) square white craft foam
- White pom-poms: four ½" (1.3 cm), eight 3 mm
- Acrylic paints: white, medium green, yellow, pink, blue, light green, lavender, turquoise

- Paintbrushes: No. 8 flat, 1" (2.5 cm) sponge, fine liner
- Water-base acrylic sealer
- Miscellaneous items: fine sandpaper, tack cloth, pencil, tracing and white transfer paper, stylus, scissors, ruler, paint palette, white craft glue

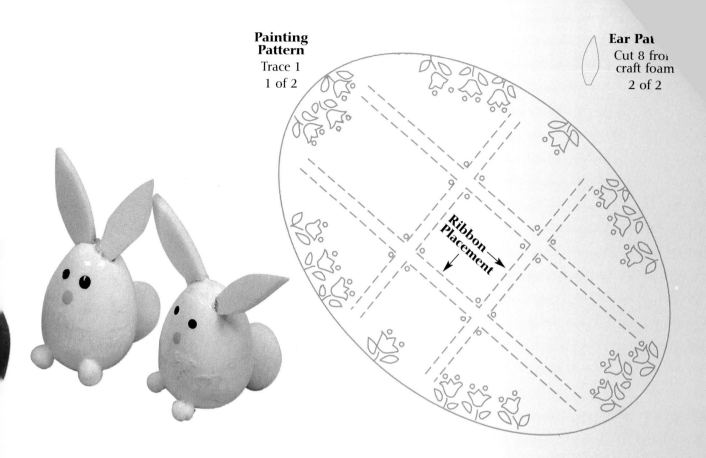

Ribbon Placement

1 *Preparation:* Refer to Painting Instructions and Techniques on page 160. Sand wooden plaque and eggs smooth. Also sand wide end of eggs to flatten so they will stand upright; remove sanding dust with tack cloth. Apply acrylic sealer with sponge brush to plaque and eggs; let dry.

2 *Basecoating:* Use sponge brush and medium green paint to base-coat plaque top and edges. Use No. 8 brush to basecoat 4 eggs white, and 1 egg each yellow, pink, blue and turquoise.

3 *Pattern:* Trace the painting pattern. Using transfer paper and stylus, transfer pattern to plaque. From green ribbon, cut 2 each of the following lengths: 2³/4" and 4" (7 and 10 cm). Refer to the pattern to first glue long, then short ribbons, crisscrossing on the gameboard.

4 *Painting Flowers:* Refer to the photo and Step 4 illustration to use liner brush to paint pink, yellow and lavender flowers with light green stems. Use stylus tip to dot contrasting colors above flowers and lavender dots in corners where ribbons intersect.

5 *Bunnies:* Refer to the photo to dot black eyes and a pink nose. Glue 2 small pom-pom feet to bottom front and large pom-pom tail to bottom back. Use the bunny ear pattern to cut 8 ears; glue ears to head.

6 *Eggs:* See the Step 6 illustration to use liner brush to paint decorations on the 4 Easter eggs in the appropriate colors, or as desired. Paint stripes or lines first; then add dots last. Use sponge brush to apply 2 coats of sealer to gameboard, bunnies and eggs.

63

Decorate a grapevine wreath with tulips made of craft foam, and it will last all spring long, without ever losing a petal or leaf. The tulip egg designs are craft foam cut with pattern–blade scissors and punched holes.

List of Materials

- 9" x 12" (23 x 30.5 cm) or 11½" x 17½" (29.3 x 44.3 cm) craft foam sheets, 1 each: big green, big yellow, big purple, little pink, little white

- Fifteen 18" (46 cm) green cloth-wrapped floral stems
- 2 or 3 pattern-blade scissors
- Hole punch
- Thick white craft glue
- Spanish moss

- 18" (46 cm) oval grapevine wreath
- Pattern Page 164
- Miscellaneous items: tracing paper, pencil, wire cutters, scissors

1 *Preparation:* Trace the 3 patterns to tracing paper with pencil, and cut out. Trace the patterns to the back side of foam, which is a little smoother and easier to trace on. See the Step 1 illustration for how to group the petals while tracing, for easier decorating later on. Cut floral stems in 3 with wire cutters to make 6" (15 cm) pieces.

2 *Cutting:* See the Cutting Chart for how many of large and small petals to cut from which color. Cut out all small petals, and plain large petals. Leave large petals that will be decorated uncut. Trace 20 leaves to green foam; cut out.

3 *Decorations:* Cut strips with pattern-blade scissors and punch holes from extra craft foam. For purple tulip eggs, cut 3 strips of white craft foam. Punch holes and cut strips of yellow and purple to decorate white tulip eggs. Cut 3 strips each of purple and white to decorate pink tulip eggs. Cut strips of purple and pink to decorate yellow tulip eggs.

4 *Large Petals:* Place faceup 4 colors of foam that have large petal patterns traced on the back. Refer to the photo and the Step 4A illustration to glue foam strips and holes onto front side of foam with craft glue; let dry. After glue dries, cut some small petals from decorated strip, if desired, for a totally decorated tulip egg—2 per egg. Cut out large petal shapes as shown in 4B.

5 *Egg Tulip Assembly:* Make each egg tulip with the same color foam using 1 large decorated petal, 1 plain large petal and 2 small petals. Glue 2 small petals on either side and floral stem in the center, to back side of large decorated petal. See the Step 5 illustration to glue on top of the plain large petal.

6 *Tulip Assembly:* Make each tulip with the same color foam using 1 large petal and 3 small petals. Glue 2 small petals on either side and floral stem in the center, to front side of large petal. Glue 1 small petal on top in the center, covering up the floral stem.

7 *Finishing:* Glue Spanish moss to the lower part of the wreath. Glue a floral stem to the back of each craft foam leaf. Refer to the photo to insert egg tulips, tulips and leaves into the moss and wreath as desired.

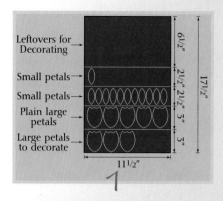

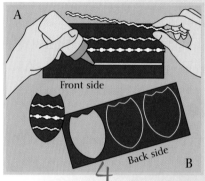

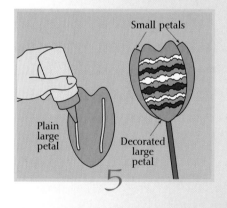

Cutting Chart

Large Petals To Decorate	Plain Large Petals	Small Petals	Color	End Result	
				Egg Tulips	Tulips
2	7	19	Yellow	2	5
3	5	12	Purple	3	2
2	6	16	Pink	2	4
5	5	10	White	5	0
12	23	57	Total	12	11

Fun for the yard, flower bed, or to show where the Easter egg hunt begins, this quick little sign can brighten up lots of different places. If there's no spot in the yard, cut off the dowel below the arrow and add a wire hanger for a fun doorhanging.

List of Materials

- 6" x 24" (15 x 61 cm) of ¾" (2 cm) pine
- 3 ft. (0.95 m) of ½" (1.3 cm) wood dowel
- 2 wood eggs, 2¼" (6 cm)
- Acrylic paints: black, white, gray, light blue, pink, yellow
- Paintbrushes: ¼" (6 mm) flat, liner, 1" (2.5 cm) sponge, stencil (or makeup sponges)
- ½" (1.3 cm) checkerboard stencil
- ⅓ yd. (0.32 m) yellow satin ribbon, ⅜" (1 cm) wide
- Scroll saw
- Drill and ½" bit
- Wood glue
- Pattern Sheet
- Miscellaneous items: tracing paper, pencil, sandpaper, tack cloth, graphite paper, stylus, paint palette, scissors

1 *Preparation:* Refer to Painting Instructions and Techniques on page 160. Let paint dry between coats and colors. Trace patterns to tracing paper and cut out. Place patterns on pine, and trace around them. Cut out bunny and arrow with scroll saw.

2 *Drilling:* Use ½" bit to drill a hole through each egg from narrow to wide end. Drill holes completely through arrow and ½" (1.3 cm) into bunny as indicated on pattern and shown in the Step 2 illustration. Sand bunny, arrow and eggs smooth; remove sanding dust with tack cloth.

3 *Basecoating:* Use 1" (2.5 cm) sponge brush to basecoat arrow and dowel with white and bunny with gray. Basecoat 1 egg with pink and the other with yellow.

4 *Arrow:* Place checkerboard stencil over straight end of arrow. Use stencil brush or makeup sponge and blue paint to dry-brush the squares. Carefully lift and reposition stencil as needed to do the entire arrow front, aligning with previously painted squares. Transfer "BUNNY TRAIL" and bunny details to arrow and bunny with graphite paper and stylus. Paint "BUNNY TRAIL" on arrow with gray and ¼" (6 mm) flat brush.

5 *Bunny:* Use stencil brush and white paint to dry-brush the outer edges of bunny. Paint the bunny's tail white with ¼" (6 mm) brush. Make a white dot for the eye; add a black dot partially covering the white one. Use the liner brush and black paint to make a small black curved line over the eye dots, and add lashes and whiskers. Paint the nose pink.

6 *Pink Egg:* Use the ¼" (6 mm) flat brush to paint a white band around the center of the pink egg. Paint squiggly white lines with the liner brush around egg, above and below the band. Make white dots along edges of the white band. See the Step 6 illustration to make 2 light blue dots side by side in center of white band; use the tip of the liner brush to join dots, pulling bottom edges together to form heart.

7 *Yellow Egg:* Refer to the photo to make clusters of 4 blue dots on the yellow egg. Add a pink dot in the center of each 4-dot cluster to form a flower.

8 *Assembly:* Slide arrow onto dowel with dowel extending 7" (18 cm) above top of arrow. Mark the placement lightly with a pencil. Slide the arrow above the mark and apply glue to the dowel where the arrow will be placed, as shown in the Step 8 illustration. Slide arrow over glued area and let dry. Slide eggs onto dowel above arrow; mark and glue same as for arrow. Apply glue to top end of dowel and slide bunny onto dowel. Tie yellow ribbon around bunny's neck.

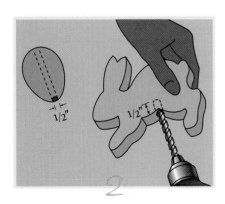

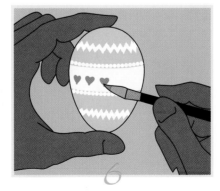

SPRINGTIME
Lamb

*C*lothe a premade lamb in a gown lush with flower blossoms, then complete the attire with an apron and bonnet sewn from a Battenberg doily and towel.

List of Materials

- 14″ (35.5 cm) muslin lamb* with ½″ (1.3 cm) copper bell
- Battenberg tea towel*
- 6″ (15 cm) square fabric/Battenberg doily*
- ½ yd. (0.5 m) floral print cotton fabric, 45″ (115 cm) wide

- 1 yd. (0.95 m) each coordinating satin ribbon: ⅛″ (3 mm), ⅜″ (1 cm)
- Needles: sewing, large-eyed
- Hot glue gun

- Pattern Page 163.
- Miscellaneous items: pencil, scissors, tracing paper, yardstick, straight pins, sewing machine and matching threads, 2 tea bags, measuring cup, iron

*(See Sources on pg. 175 for purchasing information.)

1 *Cutting & Preparation:* Trace the bodice and apron bib patterns; cut out the bodice as indicated. From floral print fabric, cut two 10″ x 22″ (25.5 x 56 cm) skirts and two 7½″ x 14″ (19.3 x 35.5 cm) sleeves. Sew fabrics right sides together with a ¼″ (6 mm) seam allowance, unless otherwise indicated.

2 *Bodice & Sleeves:* Pin bodice pieces along neck and stitch around neck opening. Cut close to stitching as shown in the Step 2 illustration; turn and press. Press one 7½″ (19.3 cm) edge of each sleeve under ¼″ (6 mm); topstitch to hem. Machine-gather opposite edges, pull gathers to fit bodice armholes and stitch sleeves to bodice.

3 *Skirt:* Machine-gather one 22″ (56 cm) edge of each skirt. Pull gathers to fit bottom edges of bodice; stitch skirts to bodice. Sew skirt side and bodice underarm seams; turn. Turn bottom skirt edge under ¼″ (6 mm) twice, and topstitch hem.

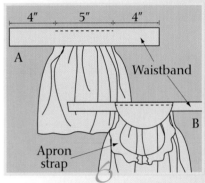

4 *Finishing Dress:* Cut ⅛″ (3 mm) ribbon into 3 equal pieces. Thread 1 ribbon piece into the large-eyed needle and hand-sew running stitches 3″ (7.5 cm) from bottom of each sleeve. Place dress on lamb, then pull ribbon to gather sleeves around arms. Knot ribbon and tie small bows as shown in photo. Thread bell on remaining ribbon piece and tie around neck.

5 *Tea-Dyeing:* Place tea bags in 2 cups (500 mL) of boiling water for 3 minutes; remove. Place towel and doily in tea until desired color is achieved. Rinse under cold water, dry and press. Refer to the Tea Towel and Doily Cutting Guides to cut pieces for the bonnet and apron along the dashed lines from the tea towel and doily.

6 *Apron Skirt:* Machine-gather top edge of apron; pull gathers to measure 5″ (12.5 cm) and knot. Center apron on waistband, matching raw edges, and stitch as shown in 6A illustration.

7 *Apron Bib:* Stitch lace apron straps together along 1 short edge to make 1 long piece. Layer apron bibs, sandwiching strap ends where indicated on pattern. Stitch around bib curve; leave straight edge open and turn. Pin bib to apron waistband, matching raw edges, and stitch; see 6B illustration. Place apron on lamb; turn waistband ends under and slipstitch.

8 *Apron Ties:* Stitch apron ties together along 1 short end. Turn right side out, and press long edges in ¼″ (6 mm); topstitch close to edge. Place tie around waistband; tie bow at center back.

9 *Bonnet:* Machine-gather bonnet ¼″ (6 mm) in along curved edge; pull gathers to measure 5″ (12.5 cm). Zigzag lace brim to gathered edge, sewing lace points together at ends. Tack two 12″ (30.5 cm) lengths of ⅜″ (1 cm) ribbon to inside of bonnet for ties.

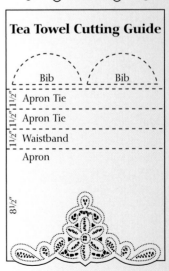

PANORAMA
Eggs

*C*ut real eggshells, then decoupage real or paper flowers around the egg opening, glue tiny silk flowers on a bed of moss, and tuck miniatures inside the egg to make these adorable spring fantasy scenes.

List of Materials

- Whole raw egg
- Acrylic paints: color for inside of egg and bead hanger
- Small paintbrush
- Moss: green, Spanish (for silk flower egg only)
- Miniatures: 2 birds, 2 bunnies, 3 eggs

- Trims: mini silk flowers with leaves; small pressed dried flowers such as dianthus, geraniums, violets, marigolds, and ageratum with leaves; mini floral paper cutouts from gift wrap
- For hanger: 4″ (10 cm) satin ribbon, ⅛″ (3 mm) wide, and large-hole bead

- For egg base: ½″ (1.3 cm) white plastic ring or clear 35 mm film canister lid
- Glues: white craft, hot glue gun
- Miscellaneous items: small sharp scissors, pencil

1 *Eggshell:* Mark a 1¼" x 1½" (3.2 x 3.8 cm) oval lengthwise on side of the egg. Use scissors to puncture center of oval and cut out as shown in the Step 1 illustration. Carefully remove inside of egg and rinse shell with water; let dry. Paint inside of egg with desired color, and let dry.

2 *Pressed Flower Egg:* Brush thinned glue (add water to glue), a small area at a time, around oval opening. Refer to the photo to slightly overlap flowers and leaves around the opening. Fill in with leaves and small ageratum. For marigolds, layer 4 petals on the glue. Brush petals with glue and add 3 petals on top. Repeat to add 2 more petals. Apply 2 coats of thin glue on entire outer eggshell to protect surface and add a gloss.

3 *Floral Paper Cutout Egg:* Carefully cut 1" to 2" (2.5 to 5 cm) floral motifs from gift wrap. Brush thinned glue on back of motifs and arrange around oval opening, overlapping and extending opening slightly; see the Step 3 illustration. See Step 2 to apply 2 coats of glue over gift wrap cutouts.

4 *Silk Flower Egg:* Hot-glue a ¾" (2 cm) border of Spanish moss around oval opening. Glue silk mini flowers and leaves onto the moss.

5 *Panoramas:* Determine bottom of egg and hot-glue layer of moss in center. Hot-glue desired miniature(s) onto moss; see the Step 5 illustration.

6 *Base or Hanger:* Hot-glue 35 mm film canister lid or plastic ring to bottom of egg. For hanger, paint the bead with a coordinating color. Fold ribbon in half and hot-glue ends into bead hole. Hot-glue bead to center top of egg.

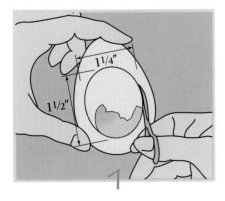

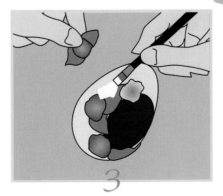

71

Easter Easter Easter Easter Easter Easter Easter

TEE TIME *Clock*

$\mathcal{A}$ golf ball and tee adorn an elegant faux finish clock to remind Mom or Dad of upcoming tee times. Although the clock won't improve scores, it's guaranteed to keep their favorite sport in the "fore"front of their minds.

List of Materials

- Wood oval mantel clock, 2½" x 6⅝" x 8½" (6.5 x 16.5 x 21.8 cm)
- 3½" (9 cm) ivory and gold clockworks with Arabic numerals
- White golf ball and tee
- Waterbase wood sealer
- Faux finish kit: bronze/silver/brown glazing is shown, but crackling, marbling, verdigris, rust or any other finish appropriate for wood may be used
- Paintbrushes: 1" (2.5 cm) sponge, No. 6 flat
- Spray adhesive
- ¼" x ¾" (6 mm x 2 cm) wood letters: 3 E; 1 each I and M
- White acrylic paint
- Satin finish acrylic varnish
- Black fine-point permanent-ink marker
- Wood glue
- Miscellaneous items: hacksaw or band saw, sandpaper, tack cloth, sheet of plain paper, pencil, scissors, paint palette

1 *Preparation:* Use the hacksaw or band saw to cut the golf ball and tee in half. Use 1 of the golf tee halves as a pattern and trace around it 9 times with a pencil onto the sheet of plain paper. Use the No. 6 flat brush to paint the wood letters and the golf tee halves white.

2 *Sealing:* Apply wood sealer to the clock with the sponge brush; let it dry. Sand the clock lightly; remove dust with tack cloth.

3 *Basecoating:* Follow the manufacturer's instructions in the faux finish kit to basecoat the clock using the sponge brush or other recommended applicator. In the photo a bronze paint was used. Let dry between paint and color, unless otherwise indicated.

4 *Tee Stencils:* Place the clockworks on the clock and lightly mark on the top and sides of the clock where it will be; see the Step 4 illustration. Cut out the paper tees; spray the wrong side of the traced tees with spray adhesive. Refer to the photo to place the paper tees on the clock, adhesive side down. Arrange 3 tees around where the clockworks will be, and the remaining 6 on the side and top edges.

5 *Faux Finish:* Apply remaining faux finish products to the front of the clock over the paper tees. Remove the paper tees, as shown in the Step 5 illustration. Repeat on the sides and the back of the clock.

6 *Finishing:* Apply varnish with the sponge brush to the entire clock, the letters and the 2 tee halves following manufacturer's instructions. Outline the tee designs on the clock with the permanent marker. Insert the face and clockworks into the clock.

7 *Gluing:* Refer to the photo and the Step 7 illustration to position and use wood glue to glue the 2 tee halves to the bottom left of the clock, making a T. Repeat to glue the letters, spelling out "Tee Time." Glue half of the golf ball to the right front of the clock.

Personalized mouse pads are all the rage, and here is a clever way of using a photocopier to make your own mouse pad from a favorite photo.

List of Materials

- 9" x 12" (23 x 30.5 cm) muslin
- 9" x 12" (23 x 30.5 cm) freezer paper
- Black and white photocopy machine
- 4" x 6" (10 x 15 cm) or 5" x 7" (12.5 x 18 cm) photo
- Fabric or acrylic craft paints, in colors to match photo
- Colorless medium or extender (for acrylic or fabric paints)
- Paintbrushes: a variety of flat, round and liners
- Flexible fabric-covered mouse pad, no larger than 8½" x 11" (21.8 x 28 cm)
- 9" x 12" (23 x 30.5 cm) fusible web
- Black fabric or permanent-ink marker
- Miscellaneous items: iron, scissors, ruler, pencil, paint palette

1 *Preparation:* Lay muslin on flat, hard work surface. Place freezer paper over the muslin, shiny side down. Use a dry iron set on a medium temperature to iron the freezer paper to the muslin until it bonds.

2 *Cutting:* Use the ruler and pencil to mark the freezer paper/muslin piece to 8½" x 11" (21.8 x 28 cm); and cut out. This piece will go through the photocopy machine, so the measurements must be exact.

3 *Testing:* Put the photo in the black and white photocopy machine. Make a test print copy on regular paper, manually feeding the paper through the machine. Note which side of the paper is right side up, as it is fed through the copier. Make any adjustments, such as enlarging, darkening and lightening, or setting the machine on auto or photo.

4 *Copying:* Refer to the Step 4 illustration when you are satisfied with the photocopy quality on regular paper. Manually feed the freezer paper/muslin piece through the copier, with the muslin side as the right side. Let the photocopied fabric cool off; leave the freezer paper on until you are done painting.

5 *Painting:* Thin acrylic paints with medium or fabric paints with extender, because you are just tinting the photo, rather than painting it. Start at 1 side or the top, and color in the muslin photocopy to match the photo. You will not need to do much shading or highlighting, because of the gray tones from the photocopy. Let dry.

6 *Cutting:* Place the mouse pad on the fusible web and tinted muslin photocopy, and trace around each lightly with a pencil. See the Step 6 illustration to cut around traced line on fusible web and muslin photocopy to get mouse pad shape.

7 *Fusing:* Remove freezer paper backing from muslin photocopy. Follow manufacturer's instructions to fuse web to wrong side of muslin photocopy. Place the mouse pad faceup on a flat work surface. Remove paper backing from fusible web and fuse muslin photocopy to right side of mouse pad as shown in the Step 7 illustration.

8 *Finishing:* Use marker and a ruler to make a ⅛" (3 mm) border all around the edge of the mouse pad. This photocopy technique will work for a variety of other uses. Photocopy onto fabric/freezer paper combinations that can be used for quilt blocks, pillows, in memory books, picture frames, lamp shades, etc. The freezer paper simply makes the fabric stiff enough for it to go through a photocopy machine. Always check with photocopy machine owners for permission to use fabric in their machines.

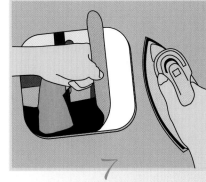

Moms and dads alike will love wearing and using these cheery grill accessories. The chicken design is simple to paint; you make dots with the end of a paintbrush handle.

List of Materials

- Director's chair with natural cotton canvas seat and back
- Black canvas chef's apron
- Wood-handled grill utensils
- 3" x 5" (7.5 x 12.5 cm) white round crock

- ½" (1.3 cm) checkerboard stencil
- Acrylic paints for utensils and crock, fabric paints for chair and apron: black, red, gold, buttermilk
- Paintbrushes: No. 4, 8 and 1" (2.5 cm) flat, fine liner

- Matte acrylic spray finish
- Miscellaneous items: tracing and graphite paper, pencil, paint palette, masking tape, cardboard, colored chalk, stylus or empty ballpoint pen, ruler

1 *Patterns and Preparation:* Trace the patterns onto tracing paper. Refer to the photo for chicken positioning and to page 160 for Painting Instructions and Techniques. Use masking tape and fasten chair pieces and apron to heavy cardboard. On the wrong side of patterns, rub over pattern lines with chalk. Transfer to fabric by placing patterns chalk side down and tracing over lines with stylus.

2 *Chair Back:* Use the No. 4 flat brush to paint chicken bodies black. Either leave the dots and eye unpainted, or paint the entire body and add buttermilk dots and eyes later. Use the liner brush to paint the combs and wattles red, and beaks and feet gold. Lightly mark off a ¼" (6 mm) border with ruler and pencil along the top and bottom edges of the chair back, and paint red with the No. 8 brush.

3 *Chair Seat:* Refer to the photo and Step 3 illustration for border design. Use the ruler and pencil to lightly mark 2 rows of 1" (2.5 cm) squares on front and back edges of seat. Use masking tape and ruler to mark off three ⅜" (1 cm) stripes. Use the 1" (2.5 cm) brush to paint every other square red; let dry. Use No. 8 brush and black to paint 2 stripes with a blank stripe between; let dry.

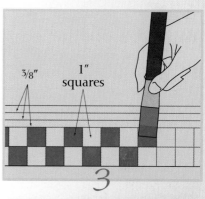

⅜"   1" squares

3

4 *Apron:* Repeat Step 2 to paint chicken, only use buttermilk for the body, and add black dots and eye as shown in the Step 4 illustration. It may take more than 1 coat of paint to cover black fabric. If desired, lightly mark off a ⅜" (1 cm) border with ruler and pencil along pocket, or on apron to look like a pocket. Paint border red with No. 8 brush.

5 *Crock:* Lightly mist the outer edge with water, and transfer 2 small chickens with graphite paper and stylus. Repeat Step 2 to paint the chicken. Use No. 8 flat brush, red paint and checkerboard stencil to make border around top of crock. Let dry; spray with several coats of acrylic finish, following manufacturer's instructions.

4

6 *Utensils:* Basecoat the handles with buttermilk or black using No. 8 brush. Accent top and bottom of handles with red and No. 4 brush. Add gold bands with fine liner. Make contrasting dots on handles. Let dry; spray with several coats of acrylic finish.

Small Chicken Pattern
Trace 2, reversing 1, for crock
2 of 2

Large Chicken Pattern
Trace 1 for apron;
trace 2, reversing 1, for chair
1 of 2

DRAGONFLY
Treasure Box

A simple wooden box can be stained, matted and decorated with any wooden cutout design. With the soft fabric lining it makes a perfect resting place for treasures–fishing flies, marbles, coins or jewelry.

List of Materials

- Wooden box with a picture frame opening lid, with or without hinges, 8" x 6" x 1½" (20.5 x 15 x 3.8 cm) box is shown

- Colored stain: green, blue

- Dragonfly wooden cutout

- Natural crackle mat board to fit picture frame opening–see Step 2

- Sheepskin-like fake fur to fit box interior–see Step 4

- 1" (2.5 cm) sponge brush

- Thick white craft glue or all-purpose adhesive

- ¾" x 3" (2 x 7.5 cm) leather (or brass hinges), 8 nail or screw fasteners

- Antique brass hasp and padlock

- 12" (30.5 cm) red satin ribbon, ¼" (6 mm) wide

- Waterbase clear varnish

- Miscellaneous items: soft cloth or paper towels, sandpaper, tack cloth, scissors, craft knife, pencil, ruler, piece of cardboard, hammer or screwdriver

1 *Staining:* Follow the manufacturer's instructions to apply blue stain to the box interior and sides, and wooden dragonfly cutout top and edges. Wipe off any excess with soft cloth or paper towels. Repeat to apply green stain to all lid surfaces. Sand the box, lid and dragonfly lightly, following the grain of the wood, to give an aged, stressed appearance; refer to the photo. Remove dust with a tack cloth.

2 *Mat Board:* See the Step 2 illustration to measure the picture frame opening of box lid on the back side. Use the ruler and pencil to mark the picture frame opening measurements on the mat board; use the ruler and craft knife to cut out.

3 *Varnishing:* Use the 1" (2.5 cm) foam brush to apply varnish to the right side of the mat board and all stained surfaces. Be careful not to let any drips accumulate in the picture frame opening. Let box and lid dry separately.

4 *Lining:* See the Step 4A illustration to measure the depth of the box on the inside and the interior length and width. Multiply the depth (1¼" or 3.2 cm) times 2 (2½" or 6.5 cm). Add that to the length (5½" or 14 cm) and width (7½" or 19.3 cm) to get the total length (8" or 20.5 cm) and width (10" or 25.5 cm). Cut the fake fur lining to those measurements, as shown in 4B. Mark and cut squares from the corners that measure the box interior depth.

5 *Gluing:* Apply glue to the box interior; spread evenly across the bottom using a stiff piece of cardboard. Center the fake fur lining over the glue, and press gently into place. Apply glue in the same way along the box interior sides; press and smooth the lining edges into place.

6 *Dragonfly:* Place the wooden dragonfly cutout centered on the mat board, right side up, and lightly pencil-mark the top and bottom. Place mat board in picture frame opening; move closures to hold in place. Apply glue to the back of the dragonfly; glue to the mat board between the pencil marks. Let dry; erase pencil marks.

7 *Hinges:* If your box already has hinges go on to Step 8. Measure and mark box with pencil 1¼" (3.2 cm) in from the sides on the back and lid, as shown in Step 7. Cut leather into 2 pieces ¾" x 1½" (2 x 3.8 cm). Screw or nail leather hinges onto back and lid, using 4 fasteners total on each hinge. If using metal hinges, attach in the same place.

8 *Finishing:* Measure and mark with pencil the center of box on the front and lid. Fasten the hasp onto the box and lid on those center marks. Knot the satin ribbon ends; put through the padlock keyholes, center, and knot.

Lid back side

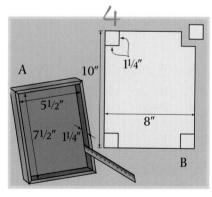

If Mom or Dad is a sports nut glued to the tube whenever a game is on, either one would appreciate this message (stitched with Mother, for Mom, of course) cross-stitched and finished as a pillow or mounted in a frame.

List of Materials

For Both Projects

- 1 skein each 6-strand embroidery floss in colors listed on Color Key
- No. 24 tapestry needle
- 4 ball buttons
- 1½ yd. (1.4 m) black grosgrain ribbon, ⅜" (1 cm) wide
- Pattern Sheet

For 12" (30.5 cm) Square Pillow

- 8" (20.5 cm) square 14-count white Aida cloth
- 45" (115 cm) cotton sports-motif fabric, ⅜ yd. (0.35 m)
- 12" (30.5 cm) square pillow form
- 1½ yd. (1.4 m) black piping

For 8" x 10" (20.5 x 25.5 cm) Framed Sampler

- 10" x 12" (25.5 x 30.5 cm) 25-count white linen
- Mat and frame of your choice
- Miscellaneous items: scissors, ruler, iron, straight pins, sewing machine and matching threads

1 *Preparation:* Refer to the Cross-Stitch General Instructions and Stitches on page 158 and the Stitch Chart on the pattern sheet to cross-stitch the design. Follow Step 1 on page 158 to find the spot to begin stitching, but make sure on the linen sampler to begin stitching over a vertical thread.

2 *Stitching Pillow:* Each square on the Chart represents 1 square of Aida cloth; use 2 strands of floss to stitch the design. Use 1 strand of red to backstitch around the letters. Sew the buttons evenly spaced on either side of "word" and "BALL."

3 *Stitching Sampler:* Each square on the Chart represents 2 threads of linen; use 3 strands of floss to stitch the design. Follow the chart to cross-stitch the word "BALL" at the bottom in red stitches, instead of the alternating black and white stitches. Use 1 strand of red to backstitch around the letters. Sew the buttons onto the sampler evenly spaced widthwise and 1³/4" (4.5 cm) below the word "BALL."

4 *Cutting:* Trim the Aida cloth to a 7" (18 cm) square, with the stitching and buttons centered within. See the Step 4 illustration to cut border strips for the pillow front and a 12" (30.5 cm) square for the pillow back from the sports motif fabric. Cut four 12" (30.5 cm) lengths of black ribbon. Stitch with right sides together, and use ¹/4" (6 mm) seams.

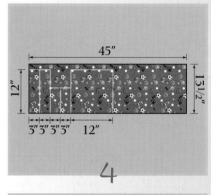

5 *Pillow Assembly:* See the Step 5 illustration to stitch the 7" (18 cm) border strips to each side of the pillow center; press seams toward the border. Stitch the 12" (30.5 cm) border strips to the top and bottom edges; press seams toward the border. Place a ribbon length centered widthwise over the top and bottom seams, and topstitch close to each ribbon edge. Repeat for the sides, with ribbons crisscrossing at the corners. Stitch piping around the outer edge of the pillow front on the right side; overlap the ends ¹/2" (1.3 cm). Stitch the pillow front to the pillow back, leaving 1 edge open. Insert the pillow form, and slipstitch the opening closed.

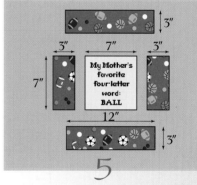

6 *Finishing Sampler:* Cut the black ribbon into two 11" (28 cm) and two 13" (33 cm) lengths. Measure ¹/2" (1.3 cm) out from stitching on the top and sides, and below the row of buttons; pin-mark. Pin the shorter lengths at the top and bottom, with the inner edges along the pin marks, and topstitch close to each ribbon edge. Repeat with the longer lengths along the sides, crisscrossing ribbons in the corners. Mat and frame as desired.

FISH PRINT
T-Shirt

Here's an inexpensive way to show off that great catch. It also works well with little catches, especially if you have a budding fisherperson who just has to take his or her fish home too.

List of Materials

- Dead fish, caught or purchased
- White or other-colored T-shirt
- Fabric paints: teal green, yellow, black, white and metallic gold

- Paintbrushes: 1" (2.5 cm) flat, liner or small touch-up
- Mister or atomizer bottle with water

- Miscellaneous items: dish soap, paper towels, large dish towel rags, newspaper

1 *Preparation:* Wash and dry T-shirt as you will after wearing; do not use fabric softener. Clean and wash the fish, using dish soap and water. Dry thoroughly with paper towels. Fold and insert the dish towel (or layer dish towels) between the front and back of the T-shirt, behind where the fish print design will go. This will absorb any excess paint during printing.

2 *Painting:* Lay fish on a few layers of newspaper in the opposite direction from how you want it printed on the shirt. Lay fins flat; do not apply paint underneath them. Use the 1″ (2.5 cm) flat brush to paint a fairly thick coat of teal green paint on the top half of the fish, head, fins and tail; refer to the photo. Paint the belly yellow, blending the colors where they meet. Paint the fish side completely, all the way up to the fish edges and fins.

3 *Positioning:* Lay out a fresh layer of news-papers in a clean work area. Place the fish on the clean newspaper, painted side up. Roll up clean paper towels, and tuck them under the edges, as shown in the Step 3 illustration, to keep the fish from rocking during the printing process. Mist the fish with the water atomizer to keep the paint moist.

4 *Printing:* See the Step 4 illustration to lay the T-shirt, with the front side down, over the fish. Be careful not to shift the T-shirt. Press down on the back of the T-shirt to help transfer the fish image onto the front of the T-shirt. You may be tempted to lay the T-shirt flat and print the fish onto it, but because the fish is 3-dimensional, it works best to lay the T-shirt on it, letting it drape around and over the fish edges.

5 *Second Printing:* Carefully lift the T-shirt straight up and off the fish. Hang up or lay the shirt flat, painted side up, and let the first printing dry for about 15-20 minutes. In the meantime, clean the fish with dish soap and water again. It is not necessary to remove all the paint, but scrubbing it out of the scales and the eye lines and other crevices will produce a second printing as clear as the first. When the first print is dry to the touch, repeat Steps 2 through 4 to print another fish. If additional prints are desired, repeat Step 5 again.

6 *Touch-Up:* Use the small liner brush to touch up any areas that are too lightly painted or missed. Blend in the area between the yellow and green paint, if necessary. Paint in the eye with a black circle. Refer to the photo to make a white dot and highlight line. See the Step 6 illustration to make a ring of metallic gold around the black pupil; you may also use a fabric marker.

7 *Finishing:* Follow the fabric paint manufacturer's instructions to iron the T-shirt and heat-set the paint, if necessary. A blue gill was used in the model; any type of fish will work. Simply use paints that represent the colors of the fish, or be creative and use any colors that you like.

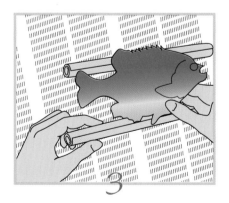

3

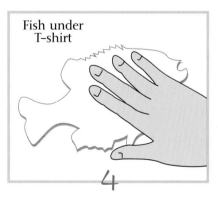

Fish under T-shirt

4

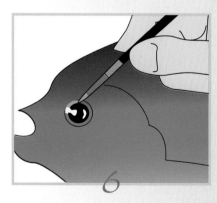

6

83

COPPER FISH
Frame

A faux-finish frame accented with copper fish and wire spotlights Dad's favorite photo.

List of Materials

- 7½" x 8" (19.3 x 20.5 cm) unfinished wood frame
- Palette knife
- Decorating medium or gesso
- Medium green acrylic craft paint
- 1" (2.5 cm) flat paintbrush
- Copper antiquing glaze and metallic wax finish

- 6" (15 cm) square 40-gauge copper foil
- 5⁄8 yd. (0.6 m) 18-gauge copper wire
- Eight ½" (1.3 cm) nails
- Miscellaneous items: comb, soft cloth, tracing paper, pencil, scissors, carbon paper, stylus, towel, hammer, wire cutters, needlenose pliers

1 *Texturizing:* Use the palette knife to cover the front and sides of the frame with decorating medium. Run a comb through the paste, creating a wave pattern; refer to the photo. Let medium dry according to the manufacturer's instructions.

2 *Painting:* Use 1" (2.5 cm) brush to paint medium green onto the textured front, back and edges of the frame.

3 *Antiquing:* Follow the manufacturer's instructions to use copper antiquing glaze and metallic wax. Thin a small amount of copper antiquing glaze and lightly brush it over the front and sides of the frame. Wipe off excess with a soft cloth. Apply the copper metallic wax to the raised areas of the frame, using your finger or soft cloth.

4 *Pattern:* Trace the fish pattern to tracing paper, and cut out. Trace the pattern 3 times onto the copper foil using carbon paper and a stylus or empty ballpoint pen. Place the foil on a towel on a work surface, right side down.

5 *Copper Fish:* Outline the fish and draw the details with the stylus, pressing hard into the copper to emboss it as seen in the Step 5 illustration. Cut out the fish with scissors. Refer to the photo to arrange the 3 fish on the frame, embossed side facing up. Attach each fish with a ¹⁄₂" (1.3 cm) nail at the eye and the tail.

6 *Seaweed:* Cut three 7" (18 cm) lengths of the copper wire. Use the needlenose pliers to curl both ends of the wire. Cut a ¹⁄₂" x 1¹⁄₂" (1.3 x 3.8 cm) strip from the copper foil for the band. Lay the 3 lengths of wire on the right side of the frame, as shown in the Step 6 illustration. Bend the copper foil strip over the wire, securing to the frame with a nail on each side.

Fish Pattern
Trace 1, cut 3 from copper
1 of 1

$\mathcal{J}$ust some taffetta ribbon and gathering stitches create a camellia as lovely as those found in a prizewinning garden. The ribbon's wire edge helps you shape perfect petals that will never drop from their stem.

List of Materials

- ⁷⁄₈" (2.2 cm) wide wire-edge taffeta ribbon: ¾ yd. (0.7 m) pink/white ombre, ½ yd. (0.5 m) green ombre
- Pearl stamen clusters
- 2 pieces 5" x 7" (12.5 x 18 cm) mat board: 1 piece uncut for frame back, 1 piece with precut oval for frame front

- ¼ yd. (0.25 m) ivory fabric
- 6" x 8" (15 x 20.5 cm) polyester fleece or batting
- Glues: hot glue gun, fabric, aerosol adhesive
- Flat paintbrush
- ½ yd. (0.5 m) ivory satin picot ribbon, ⁵⁄₈" (1.5 cm) wide

- Miscellaneous items: scissors, sewing machine, pink and green thread, sewing needle, disappearing-ink pen, chalk pencil

1 *Leaves:* Cut three 6" (15 cm) lengths of green ribbon. Fold ribbon in half widthwise, then fold the bottom corners up and down to crease, as shown in the Step 1A illustration. Stitch as shown in 1B along the creases and bottom edge, and trim the triangular corners close to stitching. Open 3 leaves, and shape.

2 *Camellia Petals:* Cut a 25" (63.5 cm) length of pink wire-edge ribbon. Mark petals on ribbon using the disappearing-ink pen as follows: three 1½" (3.8 cm), four 2" (5 cm), and five 2½" (6.5 cm). Thread needle with a long, doubled length of pink thread; knot. See the Step 2 illustration to hand-stitch around the petals along the dashed lines. Begin at 1 end, work several petals, then pull the thread to gather the ribbon tightly. Continue stitching and gathering petals to opposite end of ribbon; knot thread.

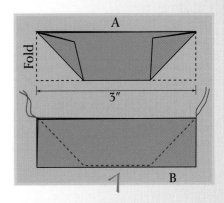

3 *Camellia Flower:* Form a circle with 3 small petals, and tack at base. Wrap 4 medium petals around center ones, tack, then repeat for the 5 large petals. Insert stamens through base, and hot-glue.

4 *Frame Fabric:* Place oval precut mat on wrong side of ivory fabric. Trace around frame and oval opening using chalk pencil. Mark fabric 1" (2.5 cm) outside traced lines, and cut as shown in the Step 4 illustration. Place frame back on wrong side of fabric and trace around it twice. Mark fabric 1" (2.5 cm) outside traced lines on 1 piece and ⅛" (3 mm) inside traced lines on the other. Spray aerosol adhesive to frame front; apply fleece. Trim even with frame edges and oval opening.

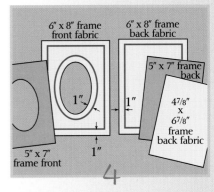

5 *Frame Front:* Place frame front, fleece side down, on wrong side of frame front fabric. Clip fabric around oval opening every ⅜" (1 cm) to within a scant ⅛" (3 mm) of mat board; see the Step 5 illustration. Using thinned fabric glue and paintbrush, apply glue around frame opening and glue fabric down a bit at a time, working on opposite edges. Apply glue at 1 outer corner and outward to the middle of each adjacent side. Wrap fabric firmly around edge of frame, pinching fabric together as shown. Repeat for remaining sides and corners. Fold pinched fabric at corners flat; glue.

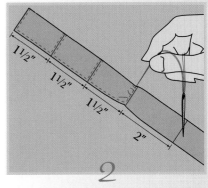

6 *Frame Back:* Spray adhesive on frame back, glue on smaller piece of frame back fabric. Center frame back, fabric side up, on wrong side of other fabric back piece. Wrap and glue sides same as for frame front. Seal raw edges of fabric with thinned fabric glue, let dry, and apply hot glue along sides and bottom edge. Center the frame front on the hot-glued frame back. Open side on top is left for inserting photo.

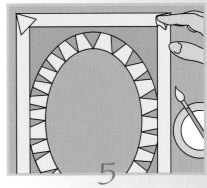

7 *Finishing:* Trim any excess at back of flower, and hot-glue to upper left corner of frame. Refer to the photo to hot-glue leaves around the flower, tucking them under petals. Cut two 3" (7.5 cm) and two 6" (15 cm) lengths of satin ribbon. Hot-glue ends of shorter ribbons together to form 2 loops; glue loops on opposite sides of flower above lower leaves. Cut Y-shapes in other ribbon ends. Refer to the photo to spot-glue as streamers, framing each side of picture opening. Hot-glue additional pearl stamens to decorate.

Mom and Dad both deserve a soothing shower or a long soak in the tub after a hard day at work. They'll love these simple-to-make bath products scented of a country garden.

List of Materials

Base Ingredients

- **Dill Soap:** two 4-oz. (125 g) bars unscented glycerin soap*

- **Black Cherry Bath Salts:** rock salt

- **Peach Preserves Shower Gel:** foaming concentrate*

- **Orange Slice Soap:** two 4-oz. (125 g) bars unscented regular or super-fatted white soap*

Oils and Fragrances

- **Dill Soap:** crushed dried dill weed, dill weed essential and jojoba oils*

- **Black Cherry Bath Salts:** glycerin, cherry fragrance oil*

- **Peach Preserves Shower Gel:** apricot kernel and peach fragrance oils*

- **Orange Slice Soap:** powdered loofah, orange fragrance oil*

Containers

- **Dill Soap:** 2" x 3" (5 x 7.5 cm) rectangular soap molds*, two 10-oz. (300 g) glass canning jars with lids

- **Black Cherry Bath Salts:** wide-mouth jar with lid; 1 yd. (0.95 m) red plaid ribbon, 1" (2.5 cm) wide

- **Peach Preserves Shower Gel:** bottle with cap

- **Orange Slice Soap:** 2 yd. (1.85 m) green sheer ribbon, 2" (5 cm) wide; 1 sheet orange tissue paper

- Miscellaneous items: small saucepan; stove; mixing spoons; green, red, yellow food coloring; measuring spoons and cups; oven-safe mixing bowls; fork; salt; food processor or cheese grater; water; wax paper; serrated knife; cutting board; toothpicks; transparent tape; ruler; scissors

*(See Sources on pg. 175 for purchasing information.)

Peach Preserves Shower Gel

Mix ¼ cup (50 mL) foaming concentrate with ¾ cup (175 mL) water, stirring gently until well blended. Add ¾ tsp. (4 mL) salt, and stir; this causes mixture to immediately thicken. Stir in until well blended and orange-colored: 1 tsp. (5 mL) apricot oil, 20 drops peach oil, and yellow and red food coloring. Pour gel into bottle and seal with cap.

Orange Slice Soap

1 *Making Soap:* Use food processor or cheese grater to shred soap into slivers. Bring ⅔ cup (150 mL) water to a boil in saucepan on stovetop. Add shredded soap; reduce to low heat. Mash and stir soap until water disappears and mixture becomes a sticky mass, about 5 minutes. Remove from heat. Stir in until color is evenly blended: 1 tsp. (5 mL) loofah, ¾ tsp. (4 mL) orange oil, ¼ tsp. (1 mL) each red and yellow food coloring.

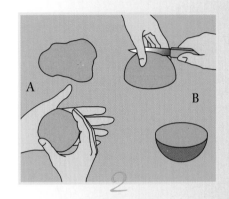

2 *Molding Soap:* When soap is cool enough to handle, divide soap in half and mold into balls with your hands, as shown in 2A. Let air-dry on wax paper for 48 hours. See the 2B illustration to cut each soap ball into 8 sections, starting from the top. Refer to the photo and use a toothpick to score lines on each side of the soap section to resemble orange slices. Separate the sections on wax paper, and let air-dry for 24 hours. Reassemble slices into balls, wrap each in tissue paper, and tape to secure. Tie a bow around each ball with 1 yd. (0.95 m) of green ribbon.

Black Cherry Bath Salts

Place 1 cup (250 mL) rock salt in large mixing bowl, and stir in 1 tsp. (5 mL) glycerin. Add 15 drops red food coloring and 30 drops cherry oil; stir with a fork until color is evenly distributed. Let the salts sit uncovered overnight; stir again, and store salts in jar with lid, or other closed container. Tie a bow around container neck with plaid ribbon.

Dill Soap

Melt glycerin soap in a saucepan on stovetop over low heat, stirring constantly until liquefied. Remove from heat, and see the illustration to stir in until well blended: 10 drops green food coloring, ½ tsp. (2 mL) each dill oil, jojoba oil and dill weed. Pour into soap molds, and let set until hardened, about 3 hours. Remove soap from molds, and cut each bar into 3 lengthwise pieces. Place soap in jars.

BEADED
Bag

What woman wouldn't love this luxurious little bag, beaded and stitched with metallic threads? It will be the perfect gift for Mom, or you should maybe even treat yourself.

List of Materials

- 1 sheet 10-mesh plastic canvas
- Kreinik's No. 32 heavy metallic braid in colors and lengths listed on Color Key
- 13 skeins DMC Cream No. 712 six-strand embroidery floss
- No. 20 tapestry needle

- 4 mm pearls, 30
- 3 mm gold beads, 168
- 2 yd. (1.85 cm) ivory rattail cord
- Gold tassel
- 1 small adhesive-backed hook-and-loop circle
- Fabric glue

- Miscellaneous items: scissors, ruler, sewing needle, gold and cream thread

90

1 *Preparation:* Refer to the Plastic Canvas General Instructions and Stitches on page 158. Use scissors to cut two 70x56 bar pieces of plastic canvas. Follow the bold outline on the Stitch Chart to carefully cut out 1 heart shape from each plastic canvas piece. Cut 2 yd. (1.85 m) of gold metallic braid.

2 *Stitching:* Use 1 strand of metallic braid to work the 3 designs in continental stitches in the colors shown in the Stitch Chart. Use 12 strands of cream floss to work the remainder of the design. Cut 2 yd. (1.85 m) of cream floss; fold in half to double it. See the Step 2 illustration to thread loop through the needle, then pull cut ends through the loop, to total 12 strands of floss. Work the border outside the beads with continental stitches and fill in the remaining background with Slanting Gobelin stitches.

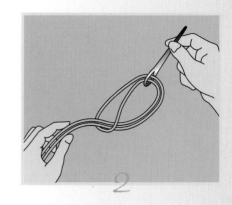

3 *Beads:* Use a regular sewing needle and gold or cream thread to work Beaded Half Cross–Stitches, attaching gold beads all around border, and 5 pearl beads in the center of each design. Knot thread ends and weave into back of stitching to secure thread.

4 *Finishing:* Tack the top of the tassel to the inside back point on 1 of the stitched hearts. Overcast top opening edges between arrows with cream floss for bag opening. Place stitched hearts wrong sides together and overcast remaining unstitched edges together. Remove paper backing and adhere hook–and–loop circles to inside top center of each heart.

5 *Handle:* Place rattail cord and 2 yd. (1.85 m) gold metallic braid together, matching at ends. Anchor 1 end, and twist cords tightly together clockwise. Carefully bring the 2 ends together, letting the cord twist around itself. Knot the cut ends to secure. Use fabric glue to glue knotted ends just inside top corners, pushing knots back under stitching.

Beaded Bag Stitch Chart

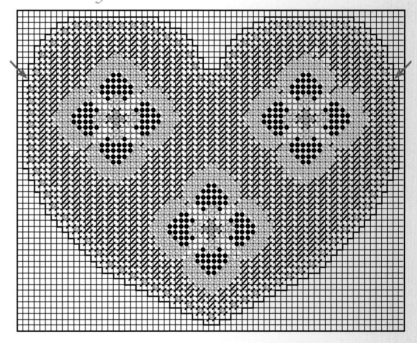

Beaded Bag Color Key

Symbol	DMC Floss # Kreinik Braid #	Color	# of Skeins/Yards
/	712	Cream Floss	12 skeins
⌐	002	Gold	5 yd. (4.6 m)
○	007	Pink	12 yd. (11.04 m)
·	042	Confetti Fuchsia	3 yd. (2.75 m)
●	034	Confetti	8 yd. (7.35 m)
●		Pearl Bead	
○		Gold Bead	

"Piece" together this Americana Wood Quilt with wood squares and star shapes covered with batting and fabric. Glue them all to a plaque, and add a ribbon border for a fast, no-sew quilt.

List of Materials

- 11″ x 14″ (28 x 35.5 cm) finished wood plaque

- Wood shapes*: fifty-eight 1″ (2.5 cm) squares; fifty-six 1/2″ (1.3 cm) squares; four 1 1/4″ (3.2 cm) stars; 1 1/2″ (3.8 cm) star

- 45″ (115 cm) cotton fabrics: 2 1/2″ x 45″ (6.5 x 115 cm) navy/ecru stars, 1 1/2″ x 30″ (3.8 x 76 cm) navy/ecru stripe, 1″ x 28″ (2.5 x 71 cm) rust/ecru stars, 1 1/2″ x 12″ (3.8 x 30.5 cm) rust/ecru stripe, 2″ x 10″ (5 x 25.5 cm) ecru/navy stars

- 2″ x 30″ (5 x 76 cm) low-loft cotton batting

- 1 1/2 yd. (1.4 m) navy grosgrain ribbon, 3/8″ (1 cm) wide

- Glues: white craft, glue stick, hot glue gun, liquid fray preventer (optional)

- Miscellaneous items: scissors, ruler, rotary cutter and mat, pencil

*(See Sources on pg. 175 for purchasing information.)

1 *Cutting & Preparation:* Cut fifty-eight 1″ (2.5 cm) batting squares. Use glue stick to glue batting to 1″ (2.5 cm) wood squares. Cut the following 1 1/2″ (3.8 cm) fabric squares: 30 navy/ecru stars, 20 navy/ecru stripe, and 8 rust/ecru stripe.

2 *Large Squares:* Place fabric square right side down on work surface. Apply glue stick to batting on wood square, and center facedown on fabric square. Use scissors to trim fabric corners diagonally 1/8″ (3 mm) from the wood corners; see the Step 2 illustration. Wrap fabric edges to back of wood square in numerical order. Secure with hot or craft glue; spot-glue corners.

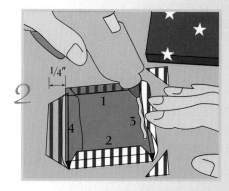

3 *Small Squares:* Cut twenty-eight 1″ (2.5 cm) squares, with a star in the center of each, from navy/ecru star and rust/ecru star fabrics. Repeat Step 2 to glue fabric squares directly to 1/2″ (1.3 cm) wood squares.

4 *Stars:* Cut five 2″ (5 cm) squares from ecru/navy star fabric. Apply glue stick to stars, and center on wrong side of fabric. Trim fabric 1/4″ (6 mm) beyond wood edges. Clip fabric at inner corners of stars and diagonally at points as shown in the Step 4 illustration. Wrap fabric to back; spot-glue edges and points with hot or craft glue.

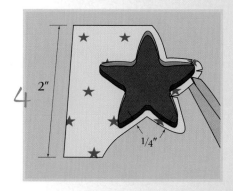

5 *Border:* Cut ribbon into two 11″ (28 cm) and two 14″ (35.5 cm) lengths. Lightly seal cut ends with craft glue or fray preventer. Use ruler and pencil to lightly draw a line 1/2″ (1.3 cm) in along each edge of plaque. Use craft glue to glue 11″ (28 cm) ribbons to board inside marked pencil lines. See the Step 5 illustration to repeat with 14″ (35.5 cm) ribbons, crisscrossing at corners.

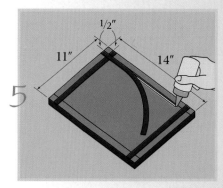

6 *Assembly:* Refer to the photo to arrange covered squares on plaque, spacing evenly and alternating the direction of striped squares. Use craft glue to glue each fabric-covered square to plaque. Glue stars diagonally in the center of blue 4-square blocks.

FOURTH OF JULY
Napkins & Holder

When friends and family gather to celebrate our nation's birthday, you can set a patriotic table. This casual dining idea is easy to make with the pot's design decoupaged on, and the napkins' edges pinked and finished with fray preventer.

List of Materials

For 4 Napkins & Napkin Rings, 1 Utensil Holder

- 45″ (115 m) cotton fabric: 1 yd. (0.95 m) patriotic print with ⅝″ to 3″ (1.5 to 7.5 cm) motifs
- 6″ (15 cm) clay pot
- Acrylic craft paints to coordinate with fabric: white, blue, red and gold
- Paintbrushes: 2″ (5 cm) sponge, small flat fabric, liner
- Glues: decoupage, white craft
- Exterior varnish
- Liquid fray preventer
- Miscellaneous items: paint palette, scissors, black fine-line permanent-ink marker, measuring tape, pinking shears, craft knife, paper towel tube

1 *Napkins:* Cut four 16″ (40.5 cm) squares of fabric with the pinking shears. See the Step 1 illustration to apply liquid fray preventer to all the napkin edges; let dry.

2 *Napkin Ring Preparation:* Cut four 1½″ (3.8 cm) lengths from paper towel tube with the craft knife; see the Step 2A illustration. Cut four 2″ x 6″ (5 x 15 cm) rectangles of fabric. Use the fabric brush to apply craft glue in small areas at a time to the outside of cardboard ring.

3 *Napkin Ring Assembly:* Center the fabric length-wise onto the ring and smooth the fabric, overlapping the ends; see 2B. Apply glue to the inside of the ring, and wrap the fabric around to the inside as shown in 2C. Coat the napkin rings with decoupage glue; apply 2 coats of varnish following manufacturer's instructions.

4 *Basecoating:* Use the sponge brush to basecoat the pot white; white paint keeps the clay color from showing through later. Basecoat the pot with 1 or 2 coats of blue. Let glues, paint and varnish dry between coats for all steps.

5 *Holder Design:* Cut out your choice of fabric motifs, such as the stars, buttons and hearts. Use the fabric brush to apply decoupage glue to the cutouts, and place them on the pot. Use the brush and your fingers to smooth out any wrinkles.

6 *Finishing Holder:* Use the liner brush and white to paint "God Bless America;" refer to the photo for lettering. Use the black marker and white paint and liner brush to draw small stitch lines around and on the fabric motifs. Use the sponge brush to apply 2 coats of varnish to the pot following manufacturer's instructions.

AMERICAN
Comet Topper

This colorful star-spangled comet made of felt will make you feel sky-high happy every time you pass by the door or window over which it hangs.

List of Materials

- Woolfelt®, 72" (183 cm) wide*: 3/4 yd. (0.7 m) royal blue; 1/2 yd. (0.5 m) each: red and white; 1/8 yd. (0.15 m) gold

- 1 skein each 6-strand embroidery floss to match felt: royal blue, red, white, gold

- 5 small adhesive-backed hook-and-loop circles

- Pattern Sheet

- Miscellaneous items: tracing paper, pencil, chalk pencil, string, ruler, straight pins, embroidery needle, scissors

*(See Sources on pg. 175 for purchasing information.)

Independence Day Independence Day Independence Day Independence Day

1 *Half Circles:* Lay blue felt on a flat work surface. Tie 1 end of a piece of string to chalk pencil; then knot string 7½" (19.3 cm) from chalk. Place knot 8" (20.5 cm) in from fabric edge, and draw a half circle 15" (38 cm) long as shown in the Step 1 illustration. Repeat to draw a circle 32" (81.5 cm) long, knotting the string 16" (40.5 cm) from the chalk. Repeat on red felt to draw a circle 30" (76 cm) long, knotting the string 15" (38 cm) from the chalk.

2 *Patterns:* Trace the comet trail and 5 star patterns to tracing paper, and cut out. Cut out from felt, following pattern instructions.

3 *Stitching:* See the Step 3 illustration to pin the small blue half circle on the left edge of the red half circle. Refer to page 158 for Embroidery Stitches; use 2 strands of matching embroidery floss for all stitches. Stitch all around the half circle with small running embroidery stitches. You may also machine-stitch the entire project, if desired.

4 *Comet Tail:* Place the white comet tail as shown in the photo, with the tip tucked between the red and blue half circles. Pin, and stitch in a single row lengthwise from the tip down the center of each of the 6 comet tails. Use slightly longer running stitches than in Step 3.

5 *Large Stars:* Place the 3 gold large stars on the blue half circle, as shown in the photo. Pin, and make tiny running stitches just along the star edge. Repeat with matching floss for the red, then white stars.

6 *Small Stars:* Refer to the photo to randomly place the 27 smaller stars on the white comet tail, and 2 gold stars on the blue half circle. Secure each star with a French knot in the center.

7 *Background:* Place the large blue half circle under the red half circle, and pin. See the Step 7 illustration to lightly draw with chalk 5 large scallops; they do not need to be perfectly symmetrical. Cut along the chalk line. Stitch the red half circle to the scalloped blue background. Use red running stitches along the red circle edge, gently working under the white comet tail stripes. Use blue floss to stitch along the small half circle bottom edge, following the previous line of stitching.

8 *Finishing:* Attach one half of 5 adhesive-backed hook-and-loop circles evenly around the upper edge of the topper. Attach the other half to the wall above the door or window where you will hang it. Or, you may make 2 or 3 thread loops on the back of the topper, and hang on nails.

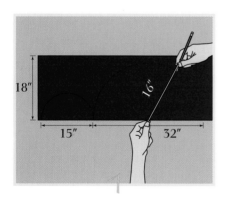

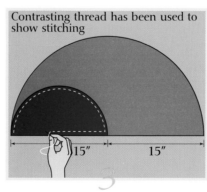

Contrasting thread has been used to show stitching

Independence Day Independence Day Independence Day Independence Day

97

Three cheers for the red, white and blue, as you sprinkle your enthusiasm with truly American colors. This European style of grouping similar flowers and foliage together emphasizes vertical lines, while the bow and streamer tie it all together.

List of Materials

- Metal watering can, 5″ (12.5 cm) high
- 3″ x 4″ x 8″ (7.5 x 10 x 20.5 cm) dry floral foam
- Silk florals: 6 red zinnias, 3 zinnia buds, 4 stems white stock, 1 blue dianthus spray with at least 5 sprigs, 1 strawberry plant

- Sheet moss
- Silk foliage: 10 green/red caladium leaves, 3 flax leaves
- 3 yd. (2.75 m) red, white and blue striped ribbon, 1½″ (3.8 cm) wide
- Green floral tape
- Greening pins

- 28-gauge wire
- Miscellaneous items: serrated knife, ruler, wire cutters, white craft glue

1 *Preparation:* Use the serrated knife to cut the floral foam block to fit in the watering can, with foam ½″ (1.3 cm) above top. Cover the foam with sheet moss, and secure with greening pins.

2 *Arranging:* Dip all floral and foliage ends in white craft glue before inserting into foam. Extend stem lengths to meet instruction measurements, if necessary, with floral tape and 28-gauge wire. Refer to the photo throughout all arranging steps below.

3 *Zinnias:* Refer to the Step 3 illustration to place the tallest zinnia in the center of the container. Its stem should be about 12″ (30.5 cm) above the foam. Cascade the remaining 5 zinnias, and 2 of the 3 buds down the center as shown.

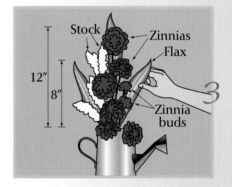

4 *Stock and Flax Leaves:* Insert the 4 white stock stems to the left of the zinnias, with the tallest blossom just below the tallest zinnia, as shown in the Step 3 illustration. Insert 1 flax leaf directly behind the tallest zinnia, keeping the height also at 12″ (30.5 cm). Place the remaining 2 flax leaves approximately 8″ (20.5 cm) above the foam on either side of the center leaf.

5 *Caladium Leaves and Dianthus:* See the Step 5 illustration side view to layer the caladium leaves in tiers around the sides and back of the watering can. Cut the dianthus spray into 5 sprigs, and refer to the photo to insert them to the right of the zinnias.

6 *Strawberry Plant:* Cut the strawberry plant into 3 clusters, and insert them at the base of the arrangement, from the center front to the right side.

7 *Bow:* See the Step 7 illustration to make a 6-loop, 5″ (12.5 cm) bow with a 4″ (10 cm) left streamer and a 12″ (30.5 cm) right streamer; secure it with a wire. Slip greening pin over bow wire, and insert pin into foam at lower left of arrangement. Loop the long right streamer through the flowers, and secure with a greening pin on the right side. Insert the remaining zinnia bud beneath the bow, angling it from the center to the left side beneath the bow.

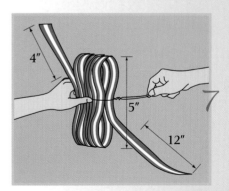

Glittering fabric paints and bright red and blue fabrics team up for an explosive impact and make these shirts sparkle like fireworks! To make children's shirts, adjust the number of stars and squares to fit the shirt front.

List of Materials

For Each Shirt
- White T-shirt
- Ultra-hold paper-backed fusible web

For Stars 'n Squiggles Shirt
- 6" x 10" (15 x 25.5 cm) blue fabric with white polka dots
- Thin expandable craft sponge

- Fabric paint: bright red, glittering gold dimensional

For Stars 'n Stripes Shirt
- Coordinating mini-print fabrics: three 4" x 10" (10 x 25.5 cm) blue prints; two 6" x 18" (15 x 46 cm) red prints
- Shiny white dimensional fabric paint

- Medium-fine opalescent glitter
- Miscellaneous items: tracing paper, pencil, scissors, light-weight cardboard, iron, pinking shears, ruler, paint palette, paper towels, T-shirt board, masking tape

Preparation & Care

Wash and dry shirts and fabrics; do not use fabric softener. Trace star pattern, and cut from cardboard to make a template. Follow manufacturer's instructions to iron fusible web to back of all fabrics. After completion, do not launder either shirt for at least 72 hours. Hand or machine wash, gentle cycle, in warm water. Cold water washing or rinsing will crack the dimensional paint. Line dry.

Stars 'n Squiggles Shirt

1 *Squares:* Cut seven 2" (5 cm) squares from polka dot fabric with pinking shears. Measure and fuse 1 square to the shirt center, 8½" (21.8 cm) below neckline. Refer to the photo to fuse remaining squares, evenly spaced, in large V shape onto shirt. Tape shirt tightly over T-shirt board.

2 *Stars:* Trace star template onto expandable sponge and cut out. Place in water to expand; dry with paper towels. Squeeze bright red paint onto palette. Refer to photo to sponge a star on a corner of each square, and 5 stars around neckline. Let dry.

3 *Squiggles:* Refer to the photo and the Step 3 illustration to use gold dimensional paint to draw squiggle lines around the stars and descending from neckline stars. Also paint small gold stars between red stars; let dry.

Star Pattern
Cut 1 from
cardboard
1 of 1

Stars 'n Stripes Shirt

1 *Stars:* Use the star template to cut from the fused fabrics: 3 from each of the 3 blue fabrics, 15 from 1 red fabric and 11 from the other red fabric. Refer to the photo and the Step 1 illustration to position stars onto shirt with top row approximately 1½" (3.8 cm) below neckline; fuse.

2 *Painting:* Outline each star with white dimensional fabric paint, completely covering raw fabric edges. While wet, sprinkle on glitter. Let dry; shake off excess glitter.

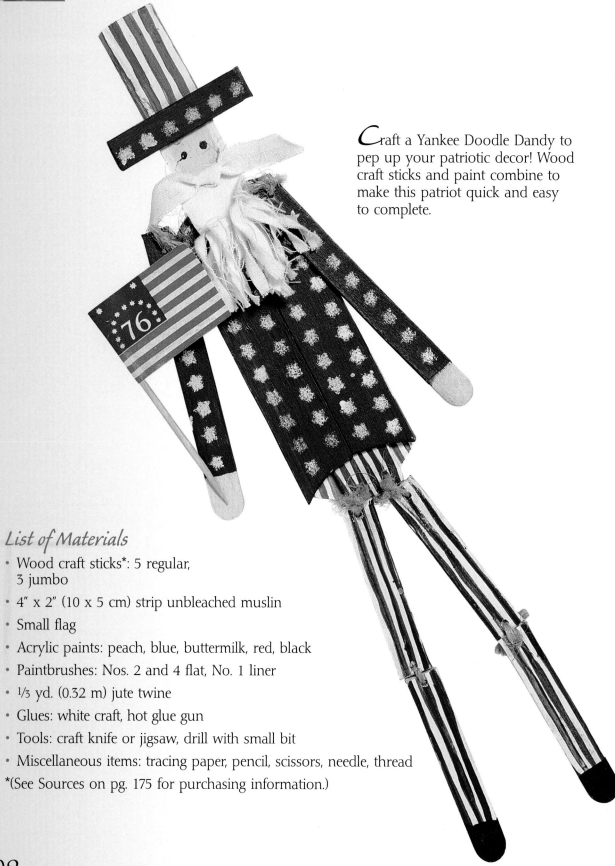

*C*raft a Yankee Doodle Dandy to pep up your patriotic decor! Wood craft sticks and paint combine to make this patriot quick and easy to complete.

List of Materials

- Wood craft sticks*: 5 regular, 3 jumbo
- 4" x 2" (10 x 5 cm) strip unbleached muslin
- Small flag
- Acrylic paints: peach, blue, buttermilk, red, black
- Paintbrushes: Nos. 2 and 4 flat, No. 1 liner
- 1/3 yd. (0.32 m) jute twine
- Glues: white craft, hot glue gun
- Tools: craft knife or jigsaw, drill with small bit
- Miscellaneous items: tracing paper, pencil, scissors, needle, thread

*(See Sources on pg. 175 for purchasing information.)

1 *Preparation:* Trace patterns, and cut out. Cut craft sticks with craft knife or jigsaw and drill holes as indicated on pattern pieces. Drill holes in only 1 body piece.

2 *Painting:* Use the No. 2 brush and peach paint to paint the face on the body piece without holes and the hands on the arms; see the Step 2 illustration. Use the No. 4 brush to paint the hair, hat, coat backs, lower body and legs with buttermilk. Paint the arms, hat brim and coat fronts with blue. Use the liner brush to paint blue stripes on the lower body and pants legs, and red stripes on hat and lower coat backs. Paint the shoes and dot eyes with black. Use the liner brush and buttermilk to paint stars on the hat brim, sleeves and coat fronts.

3 *Assembly:* Separate the strands of jute twine. To make the twine easier to thread, dip the ends in white glue and roll to a point; let dry. Attach arms to coat fronts, and upper legs to lower body and lower legs with twine; knot and trim ends on back side. Place a dab of glue on knot to secure. See the Step 3 illustration to use white craft glue and assemble Uncle Sam.

4 *Mustache & Beard:* Cut 4" x 1½" (10 x 3.8 cm) muslin strip for the beard. Use pattern to cut mustache from remaining muslin. Fold beard into 4 layers, making a 1" x 1½" (2.5 x 3.8 cm) piece. Stitch across 1 short end; clip to within ¼" (6 mm) of stitched line. Trim beard to fit face and glue. Tie a knot in the mustache center and glue above beard. Hot-glue flag to hand.

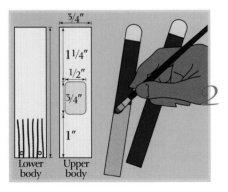

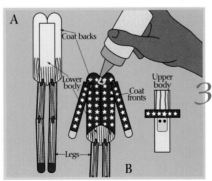

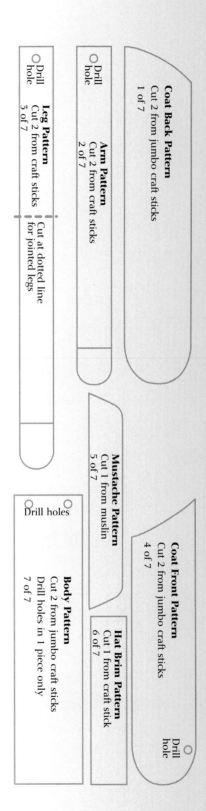

Coat Back Pattern
Cut 2 from jumbo craft sticks
1 of 7
Drill hole

Arm Pattern
Cut 2 from craft sticks
2 of 7
Drill hole

Leg Pattern
Cut 2 from craft sticks
3 of 7
Drill hole
Cut at dotted line for jointed legs

Mustache Pattern
Cut 1 from muslin
5 of 7

Coat Front Pattern
Cut 2 from jumbo craft sticks
4 of 7
Drill hole

Hat Brim Pattern
Cut 1 from craft stick
6 of 7
Drill hole

Body Pattern
Cut 2 from jumbo craft sticks
Drill holes in 1 piece only
7 of 7
Drill holes

$\mathcal{A}$ few quick coats of paint striped on clay pots bring a cast of candy corn characters to life! For a yummy filler, tuck some candy corn and peanut mix inside! It'll be all smiles for anyone who receives one of these candy cuties.

List of Materials

- Clay pot
- Acrylic paints: white, orange, yellow
- Gloss varnish
- 3/8" to 1/2" (1 to 1.3 cm) wood furniture button
- Paintbrushes: 1" (2.5 cm) flat and sponge, 1/4" (6 mm) stencil, liner
- Black medium-point permanent-ink marker
- Miscellaneous items: paint palette, blow dryer (optional), masking tape, ruler, white craft glue

1 *Basecoat:* Refer to Painting Instructions and Techniques on page 160. Let dry between each coat and color; blow-drying between will speed painting process. Use the sponge brush to basecoat entire pot and inside of rim white. Paint second coat of white on inside and outside of rim only.

2 *Stripes:* Measure where you want stripe to be on pot, and mark with masking tape. Paint center third of pot orange; paint bottom third of pot and furniture button yellow.

3 *Cheeks & Nose:* Mix a small amount of white and orange to make a lighter orange. Refer to the photo and the Step 3 illustration to use the stencil brush to dry-brush lighter orange on orange stripe for cheeks. Use the liner brush and white to paint a comma stroke highlight on 1 side of the nose button.

4 *Finishing:* Use the black marker to draw small circle eyes and a wiggly smile. Apply varnish with flat brush to entire pot and nose button following manufacturer's instructions. Glue nose button on pot.

MITTEN & GLOVE
Witches

A bit of "witch" crafting makes this frightfully delightful duo. Button fingernails on glove hands and homespun hair give the Glove Witch country charm. Her cousin, the Mitten Witch, obviously gets that shocking purple raffia hair from the other side of the family!

List of Materials

For Both Witches

- Acrylic paints: sage green, lavender, white, black
- Paintbrushes: small flat, liner
- 1 yd. (0.95 m) each embroidery floss: ecru and dark green
- 4" (10 cm) Battenberg doilies*: 1 tea-dyed round, 1 navy heart
- Wooden shapes: two 2" (5 cm) circles; 1 each ¼" (6 mm) and ½" (1.3 cm) mushroom buttons
- 1 each black witch's hat: 3" (7.5 cm) and 4" (10 cm)

- Black fine-line permanent-ink marker
- Polyester fiberfill

For Mitten Witch

- 1 large natural mitten*
- Purple raffia
- ½" (1.3 cm) plastic spider
- Uncooked rice, ¾ cup (175 mL)

For Glove Witch

- 2 small natural gloves*

- Dark hunter green dish-towel fabric*, 7" x 19" (18 x 48.5 cm)
- 10 assorted ⅜" to ½" (1 to 1.3 cm) flat green buttons
- ¼" (6 mm) wood dowel, 9" (23 cm)
- Wood craft stick
- 2" (5 cm) clay pot
- Miscellaneous items: scissors, ruler, paint palette, white craft glue

*(See Sources on pg. 175 for purchasing information.)

Mitten Witch

1 *Body:* Fill the bottom third of the mitten with rice. Fill the remainder of the mitten and thumb with fiberfill. Wrap the cuff tightly with embroidery floss and knot to form the neck. Use the small flat brush to paint a black checkerboard around the bottom of the mitten.

2 *Face:* Refer to the Painting Instructions and Techniques on page 160; let paint dry between each color and coat. Paint the wooden circle and ¼" (6 mm) button nose with the flat brush and sage green. Glue the nose to the face. Paint lavender circles for the cheeks. Make large white dots for the eyes; add a smaller dot of black inside. Dot a black wart on the nose. Use the liner brush and black paint or the marking pen to make small stars, dots near the cheeks, and mouth detail lines around the cheeks. See the Step 2 illustration.

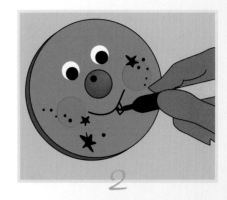

3 *Collar:* Cut a ¼" (6 mm) slit 1½" (3.8 cm) from the back edge of the doily; see the 3A illustration. Place the doily over the neck, and spot-glue; see 3B. Glue the spider to the collar.

4 *Hair:* Cut the raffia into 4" to 5" (10 to 12.5 cm) lengths and glue to the back of the head. Cut 1" (2.5 cm) pieces and glue to the forehead for bangs. Glue the head to the mitten neck. Glue the hat to the head.

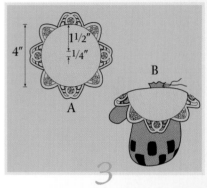

Glove Witch

1 *Painting:* Paint the face and nose lavender, and cheeks green. Glue the nose to the face. Use the liner brush and black paint or marker to make eyes with a single dot of black, dot a black wart on the nose, and make detail lines around the cheeks. Use lavender and sage green paint to paint a checkerboard design around the rim of the clay pot.

2 *Body:* Cut a slit as shown in Step 3A of Mitten Witch in from the point of the heart doily. Insert the wood dowel through the slit, letting 1" (2.5 cm) of the dowel extend above the doily. Refer to the Step 2 illustration to center and glue the craft stick just below the doily to form a "T" with the dowel. Fold the doily down over the stick and spot-glue with the point in the back. Insert and glue the opposite end of the dowel into the hole at the bottom of the clay pot. Glue the head on the top portion of the dowel so it overlaps the doily front.

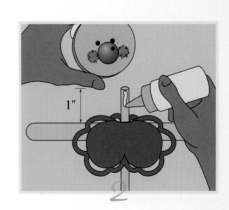

3 *Hair:* Tear the dish-towel fabric into five ½" x 19" (1.3 x 48.5 cm) strips. Fold 4 of the strips into fourths. Use the fifth strip to tie the folded strips at the center. Glue the hair and hat to the head.

4 *Hands:* Stuff the palm of each glove with fiberfill. Place a glove on each end of the craft stick. Wrap the cuff with floss and knot. Spot-glue the glove to the stick, if necessary. Glue a button to the tip of each finger.

107

Appliqué both frightful and delightful jack-o'-lanterns to make this festive fall wall hanging.

List of Materials

- 45" (115 cm) cotton fabrics: ½ yd. (0.5 m) muslin, ¼ yd. (0.25 m) each orange and green mini-prints, ⅛ yd. (0.15 m) solid black, 1 yd. (0.95 m) black border and backing print

- 22½" (57.2 cm) square low-loft quilt batting

- 2¾ yd. (2.55 m) black single-fold bias tape

- ⅔ yd. (0.63 m) paper-backed lightweight fusible web

- 7½ yd. (6.9 m) lightweight fusible tape, ¼" (6 mm) wide

- Pattern Page 168

- Miscellaneous items: tracing paper, pencil, lightweight cardboard, scissors, iron, sewing machine with zigzag stitch and matching threads, straight pins, ruler, rotary cutter and mat (optional)

1 *Preparation:* Wash and iron all fabrics. Cut a 17″ (43 cm) square from muslin. Trace the 8 patterns and cut from cardboard to make templates. Cut four 23″ (58.5 cm) lengths of bias tape and eight 23″ (58.5 cm) lengths of fusible tape. Iron 2 strips of fusible tape side by side to wrong side of bias tape and remove paper backing.

2 *Fusing:* Cut and fuse web to a 7″ x 29″ (18 x 73.5 cm) strip of green mini-print. From green fused fabric, cut three 6″ (15 cm) squares and two 4¼″ (10.8 cm) squares. Cut 2 of the 6″ (15 cm) squares and both 4¼″ (10.8 cm) squares in half diagonally to make 8 right triangles. Cut and fuse web to wrong side of 5″ x 17″ (12.5 x 43 cm) of orange fabric and 2″ x 17″ (5 x 43 cm) of solid black; refer to the Step 2 illustration.

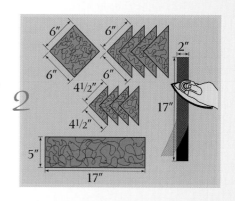

3 *Cutting:* Cut templates from fused solid black fabric in quantities as indicated on patterns. From the black border fabric, cut a 22½″ (57.2 cm) square for backing and two 3″ x 45″ (7.5 x 115 cm) strips. From each strip, cut a 3″ x 17″ (7.5 x 43 cm) piece and a 3″ x 22½″ (7.5 x 57.2 cm) piece.

4 *Diagonal Background:* Refer to photo and the Step 4 illustration to place green triangles on 17″ (43 cm) muslin square. Place 4¼″ (10.8 cm) triangles in each corner, 6″ (15 cm) triangles on each side and the 6″ (15 cm) square in the center. Remove paper backing and fuse corner triangles first, side triangles second and center triangle last.

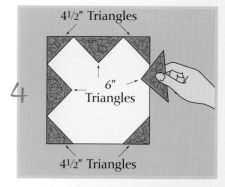

5 *Pumpkins:* Center and fuse a pumpkin in each of the 4 muslin squares. Refer to the photo to fuse stems and faces on pumpkins.

6 *Borders:* Cut two 17″ (43 cm) strips and two 23″ (58.5 cm) strips of fusible tape. Fuse a strip of fusible tape to top and bottom back edge of muslin square. Place the 17″ (43 cm) border strips at the top and bottom, ¼″ (6 mm) under muslin and fuse as shown in the Step 6 illustration. Repeat to fuse borders to sides.

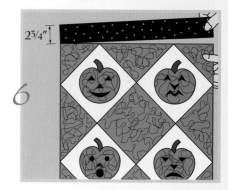

7 *Quilting:* Layer backing right side down, batting, and quilt top right side up. With black thread and medium zigzag stitch, stitch along inner edge of top and bottom borders, then side borders. With matching threads, zigzag-stitch around all fused pieces on quilt top, beginning at center and working out toward borders.

8 *Binding:* Fold 1 strip of fused bias tape in half lengthwise to encase side edge of the quilt. Beginning on front side of the quilt, fuse 3″ to 4″ (7.5 to 10 cm) of the bias tape at a time, molding it with fingers while it is warm. Do not over-press, as this will weaken the bond. Turn quilt over and repeat to fuse bias tape to back; trim ends. Repeat with second length of bias tape on opposite edge, then top and bottom edges of quilt. Stitch in the ditch close to binding edge with black thread around quilt.

A Halloween party hat becomes the backdrop for an array of autumn's colorful silk florals and natural drieds. Tie it together with a perky orange bow and a novelty mouse.

List of Materials

- 12" (30.5 cm) cardboard witch hat
- 2 yd. (1.85 m) orange satin ribbon, 1½" (3.8 cm) wide
- 1½" x 4" (3.8 x 10 cm) foam disc
- Spanish moss
- Silk florals: six 3" (7.5 cm) orange mums, gold zinnia

- spray with 2 blooms and 1 bud
- Silk wandering Jew foliage
- Blue/green berry spray
- Dried naturals: 11 stems wheat, gold mini yarrow
- Three 2" (5 cm) artificial gourd picks

- Natural raffia
- 2" (5 cm) flocked novelty mouse
- Greening pins
- 28-gauge floral wire
- Miscellaneous items: 12" (30.5 cm) square cardboard, scissors, ruler, serrated knife, wire cutters, white craft glue

1 Preparation: Cut a 10" (25.5 cm) circle from cardboard; glue to underside of the hat brim. Cut 26" (66 cm) of orange ribbon and spot-glue around base of hat crown. Twist in center to ease around curve of hat.

2 Base: Cut foam disc in half with serrated knife. Make a half-moon to fit curve of hat, as shown in the Step 2 illustration. Glue to left side of brim over orange ribbon ends. Cover foam with Spanish moss; secure with greening pins.

3 Foliage: Cut the wandering Jew foliage into the following lengths: one 13" (33 cm); three 8" (20.5 cm); and two 5" (12.5 cm). Refer to the Step 4 illustration to: insert the 13" (33 cm) stem vertically into the foam toward point of hat; insert three 8" (20.5 cm) stems trailing along the brim, 1 in front and 2 in back of hat; and insert the 5" (12.5 cm) stems in the middle pointing outward.

4 Mums: Cut orange mums into one 10" (25.5 cm), one 7" (18 cm) and four 6" (15 cm) stems. See

the Step 4 illustration to arrange mums, pushing stems into foam. Put the 6" (15 cm) stems with 2 facing forward and 2 facing back.

5 Zinnias: Cut gold zinnias with 3" (7.5 cm) stems and insert into foam base, as shown in the Step 5 illustration, looking from the top down.

6 Filler: Cut berry spray in half and insert 1 behind the mums at the base of the hat, and other across front brim; see the Step 5 illustration. Cut yarrow to fill in between flowers. Refer to the photo to insert wheat stems, following design line of the mums. Insert gourds around lower front zinnia. Glue mouse to brim on right side.

7 Bow: Take 10 strands of raffia and tie into a 9" (23 cm) 2-loop bow with 9" (23 cm) streamers. Repeat for orange ribbon; wire ribbon bow over raffia bow, and trim wires. Hook a greening pin through back of wire and see the Step 5 illustration to insert into foam at side of hat.

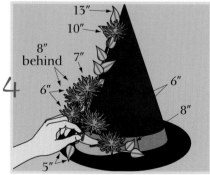

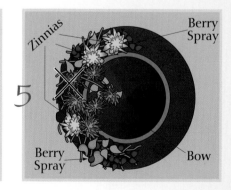

ATHERED
asks

magine two totally different masks–the elegant one is embellished with real peacock feathers, ... ary one with feathers made of craft foam.

List of Materials

For Scary Mask & Mitts

- Craft foam: 9″ x 12″ (23 x 30.5 cm) green, 3½″ x 7″ (9 x 18 cm) black, 3″ x 12″ (7.5 x 30.5 cm) purple, 2″ x 9″ (5 x 23 cm) red

- Pattern-blade scissors

- 10 wood teardrop shapes (or cut from craft foam)

- 1½ yd. (1.4 m) black elastic, ¼″ (6 mm) wide

- Black fine-point permanent-ink marker

- Paints: red spray, red dimensional

- Hot glue gun

- Pattern Pages 166-167

For Elegant Mask

- Gold plastic mask

- 1 yd. (0.95 m) yellow satin picot ribbon, ⅜″ (1 cm) wide

- Liquid fray preventer

- Feathers: 6″ (15 cm) of strung peacock blue, 3 peacock tails, 2 peacock swords (or any other feathers similar in length and shape)

- Gold sequin trim: ½ yd. (0.5 m) each: 5 mm single strand, 1¼″ (3.2 cm) wide

- 18 mm peacock blue round gemstone

- Miscellaneous items: white craft glue, tracing paper, pencil, large paper clips, newspaper, paper punch, ruler, scissors

Scary Mask & Mitts

1 *Preparation:* Trace the patterns and cut from craft foam as indicated on the pattern; patterns may be held onto the foam with paper clips. If desired, cut feathers with pattern-blade scissors. Cut elastic into the following lengths: ten 2½″ (6.5 cm), two 6″ (15 cm), one 17″ (43 cm). Spread newspapers in a well-ventilated area or outdoors; spray both sides of wood teardrops with red paint.

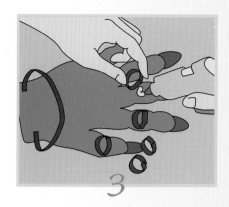

2 *Hands:* Use black marker to draw hair, knuckles and scars on foam hands. Use craft glue to attach fingernails to ends of fingers. Apply 2-3 drops of red dimensional paint to each hand to look like blood.

3 *Elastic Loops:* Hot-glue 6″ (15 cm) pieces for wrist elastic to wrong side of hands. Overlap cut ends on 2½″ (6.5 cm) elastic pieces and hot-glue together to make finger loops. Refer to the Step 3 illustration to hot-glue finger loops on wrong side of hands to fit across the middle of each finger.

4 *Mask:* Use white craft glue to glue feather foam pieces to mask: green on the bottom, and purple, then red, on top. Draw outlines and hairs on feathers to embellish. Hot-glue ends of 17″ (43 cm) elastic to each side of mask.

Elegant Mask

1 *Ribbon Ties:* Punch a hole in each side of mask next to eyes, ¼″ (6 mm) from edge. Cut ribbon in half; apply liquid fray preventer to all 4 ends. Tie a knot at 1 end of each piece. Thread unknotted end from front to back through each hole.

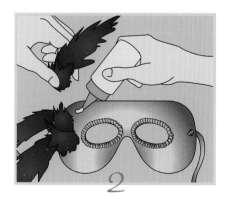

2 *Decorating:* Use white craft glue to glue the single sequin strand around each eye as shown in the photo. Begin and end at outer corner of eye. Glue groups of feathers to top corners and center top of mask, as shown in the Step 2 illustration. Glue peacock tails and swords as shown in photo, one at a time to the center top. Glue wide sequin trim across top of mask, covering feather ends. Glue gemstone to center top of mask over peacock feathers.

A simple knitting project, perfect for beginners, makes this cute pumpkin for Halloween.

List of Materials

- 4-ply worsted-weight yarn: orange, green
- No. 9 knitting needles
- 9" x 12" (23 x 30.5 cm) black felt
- Polyester fiberfill
- Pattern Pages 168–169
- Miscellaneous items: yarn needle, scissors, ruler, tracing paper, pencil, white craft glue

1 *Preparation: **Gauge:** 5 sts = 1" (2.5 cm); 7 rows = 1" (2.5 cm). Purl side is the right side, and knit side is the wrong side.*

2 *Body:* Loosely cast on 21 sts with orange yarn, leaving a 10" (25.5 cm) tail. Thread tail on yarn needle and thread back through cast-on sts, pulling yarn taut. Remove needle and let yarn tail hang.
Row 1: Purl.
Row 2: Inc 1 st in each st across.
Row 3: Purl.
Row 4: Inc 1 st in first st, *K2, inc 1 st in next st, rep from * across to last 2 sts. K1, inc 1 in last st.
Row 5: Purl.
Rows 6 and 7: Rep Rows 4 and 5.
Row 8: *K3, P1, rep from * across, ending with K1.
Row 9: Rep Row 8 until piece measures 9" (23 cm).
Row 10: With wrong side facing, *K2, K2 tog, rep from * across ending with K1.
Row 11: Purl.
Rows 12 and 13: Rep Rows 10 and 11, ending with K2.
Row 14: K1, *K2 tog, K1, rep from * across, ending with K2.
Row 15: Purl.
Row 16: K2 tog across.
Row 17: Purl.
Row 18: K1, *K2 tog, rep from * across.

3 *Stuffing:* Cut a 12" (30.5 cm) yarn tail; with yarn needle, thread through stitches on the knitting needle. Pull tight to gather; knot. Use the yarn tail to stitch the sides together to where the sts were cast on; knot. Stuff with fiberfill to desired fullness.

4 *Stem:* Cast on 12 sts with green yarn. Work in stockinette stitch (K 1 row, P 1 row) until piece measures 4½" (11.5 cm). *Next Row:* K2 tog across. Cut an 8" (20.5 cm) yarn tail and thread through stitches on needle. Pull to gather. Stitch seam together, turn and knot. Stuff top half of stem with fiberfill.

5 *Attaching Stem:* Refer to the Step 5 illustration to stitch through the front and back of the stem from inside with the threaded yarn needle. Knot tightly to bend the stem; stuff the bottom half with fiberfill. Slip stem through the top opening of the pumpkin. Pull yarn tail at the cast-on stitches to hold stem firmly in place. Slipstitch stem to pumpkin. Weave yarn tails into pumpkin and out at side; trim ends.

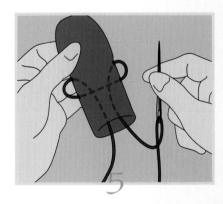

6 *Face:* Trace the face patterns onto tracing paper; cut from black felt. Refer to the photo to glue face pieces to the pumpkin.

Start with new or weathered old fence pickets and even a novice woodcutter will find these Halloween pals a cinch to make! Stand them behind the candy bowl and they'll watch for hands, big or small, trying to sneak candy before the trick or treaters arrive.

List of Materials

- 3½" x 36" (9 x 91.5 cm) wood fence picket, ½" to 1" (1.3 to 2.5 cm) thick. Check your local lumberyard or home supply center for individual pickets; sizes may vary. You may substitute 13" x 16" x ¾" (33 x 40.5 x 2 cm) pine for a fence picket.
- Acrylic craft paints: white,
black, olive green, peach, rose, red
- Paintbrushes: No. 4 flat, fine liner, 1" (2.5 cm) sponge
- Paper twist: 6" (15 cm) black, 1¼" (3.2 cm) dark green
- Spanish moss
- 1 yd. (0.95 m) jute cord

- Tools: band saw; drill with ¼" bit
- Hot glue gun
- Pattern Sheet
- Miscellaneous items: tracing and graphite paper, pencil, scissors, sandpaper, stylus, paint palette, ruler

1 *Preparation:* Refer to Painting Instructions and Techniques on page 160. Let paint dry between each coat and color.

2 *Cutting:* Trace the 2 patterns and cut out. See the Step 2 illustration to trace 1 witch and 2 ghost pattern outlines and all drill holes onto the wood picket, placing the witch at the top. Use the band saw to cut out 2 ghosts and 1 witch.

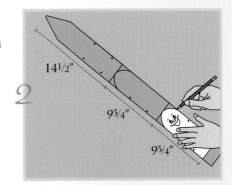

3 *Drilling:* Use the drill and ¼" bit to drill holes, 4 on the witch and 2 on opposite sides of left and right ghosts. Use sandpaper to smooth rough edges along saw cuts, drilled holes and surface, if desired. Or you can keep the surface rough, for more interest.

4 *Ghosts:* Use the sponge brush to basecoat ghosts white on back, front and edges. Use graphite paper and stylus to transfer a left ghost and right ghost face to each picket. Use the No. 4 brush and rose to paint noses and dry-brush the cheeks. Use the liner brush to paint the mouths, eyes, eyebrows and nose outline black. Dot eyes and top of noses with white highlights.

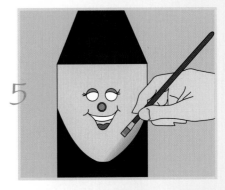

5 *Witch:* Use graphite paper and stylus to transfer face outline and nose placement to picket. Drill a shallow hole for the nose. Use the sponge brush to basecoat the face peach, and the body and hat black. Transfer the remaining face details with graphite paper and stylus. Paint the eyes and teeth white, tongue red and eyelids green. See the Step 5 illustration to shade face with green along chin. Use the liner brush and black to outline the eyes, mouth and teeth, and paint inside of mouth. Dot eyes with black for pupils.

6 *Finishing:* Center and hot-glue black paper twist across hat bottom for brim. Hot-glue 1 end of green paper twist in shallow drilled hole; bend at end to make crooked nose. Refer to the photo to glue moss hair around face.

7 *Assembly:* Cut jute cord into four 9" (23 cm) pieces; see the Step 7 illustration. Place witch between ghosts and lace a cord from back to front through 2 adjacent holes; tie bow. Dab a spot of hot glue on each jute cord end to stop fraying. Repeat for each pair of holes.

117

NO-SEW
Clown Costume

$\mathcal{I}$f making a costume fills you with fright,
try crafting with felt on this Halloween night.
Begin with a sweatshirt; add colorful trims,
ribbons and pom-poms—just follow your whims.

List of Materials

- 36" (91.5 m) felt: 1/2 yd. (0.5 m) each pink, blue
- Fusible adhesive: 1 yd. (0.95 cm) 18" (46 cm) sheet, 2 yd. (1.85 m) 1/4" (6 mm) tape
- 1 1/2 yd. (1.4 m) pleated ribbon trim, 1" (2.5 cm) wide
- 11 yd. (10.12 m) jewel-tone variegated yarn
- Fabric glue
- Sweatshirt
- 1" (2.5 cm) tinsel pom-poms
- 1/2 yd. (0.5 m) elastic, 3/8" (1 cm) wide
- Multicolored wristbands or hair scrunchies
- Miscellaneous items: scissors, yardstick, iron, disappearing-ink marker, 3" x 5" (7.5 x 12.5 cm) cardboard

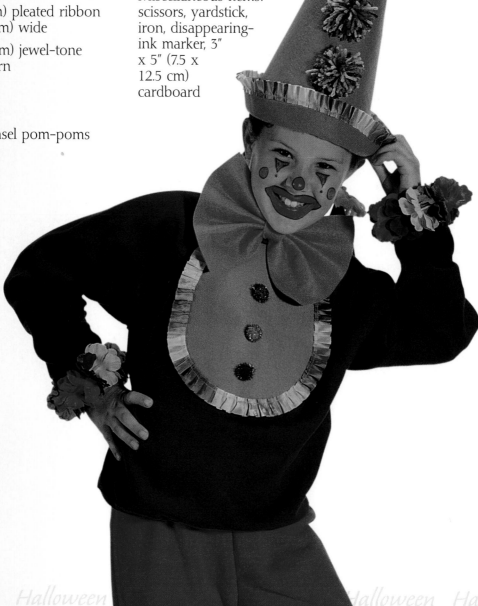

1 *Cutting:* Cut an 18" (46 cm) square each from pink and blue felt. Follow fusible web manufacturer's instructions to fuse squares together with sheet web for hat. Cut a 9" x 11" (23 x 28 cm) piece of fusible web and fuse to back side of blue felt for bib. Cut two 7" x 9" (18 x 23 cm) rectangles and one 1" x 12" (2.5 x 30.5 cm) rectangle from pink felt for bow tie.

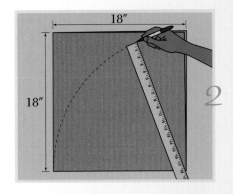

2 *Hat:* See the Step 2 illustration to use disappearing-ink marker and yardstick to draw an arc from corner to corner of the fused pink/blue felt hat square to form a cone. Cut out, and apply fusible tape along curved blue edge. Fuse pleated ribbon trim to tape, beginning 1" (2.5 cm) in from end.

3 *Hat Assembly:* Cut a 1" x 18" (2.5 x 46 cm) piece of fusible tape, and apply along 1 straight edge of hat. Wrap other straight edge around to form a cone, blue side out. Try on person's head, and fuse together so it fits. Let cool thoroughly. Refer to the photo to turn ribbon edge up 1½" (3.8 cm) for contrasting brim.

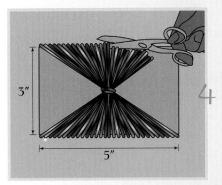

4 *Pom-Poms:* Wrap yarn around 3" x 5" (7.5 x 12.5 cm) cardboard 30 times. Tie yarn tightly at center on each side. Cut yarn along the 5" (12.5 cm) edges of cardboard, as shown in the Step 4 illustration, to make 2 pom-poms. Repeat to make 4 pom-poms and refer to the photo to glue to hat with fabric glue.

5 *Bib:* Fold fused blue bib felt lengthwise, and mark the centerline with marker. See the Step 5 illustration to mark the felt where shown with yellow dots, then draw in the dotted lines with marker. Cut bib from felt along lines. Remove paper backing and center on sweatshirt, just under ribbed collar. Trim top edge to fit collar, if necessary; fuse. Apply fusible tape on curved edge of bib, and fuse pleated ribbon trim to tape. Refer to the photo to glue front tinsel pom-poms to bib.

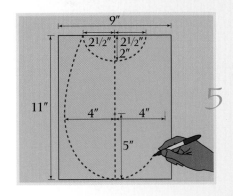

6 *Bow Tie:* Apply fusible adhesive to one 7" x 9" (18 x 23 cm) pink felt piece; fuse together with other same-size pink felt piece. Fold fused rectangle lengthwise, to make 1" (2.5 cm) accordion pleats. Tie 1" x 12" (2.5 x 30.5 cm) felt strip snugly around center on the back side to make bow tie knot. Thread elastic under the knot, tie to fit around neck, and trim ends. Slide elastic knot under felt knot to hide; spread pleats to form bow.

7 *Finishing:* Put on sweatshirt, and slide wristband or hair scrunchies over wrists. Slip bow over neck, and put on hat.

119

AINTED *Pumpkins*

$\mathcal{P}$umpkins are traditionally carved into jack-o'-lanterns for Halloween, a sometimes laborious and messy process. But here is a quick and easy way to dress up pumpkins for that special eve, and keep them inside on your table, where they won't be smashed in the morning!

List of Materials

- 3 pumpkins with stems, 6" to 9" (15 to 23 cm) in diameter
- Metallic spray paints: gold, silver, copper
- 3 yd. (2.75 m) ribbon for each pumpkin with looped bows, 1½ yd. (1.4 m) ribbon for pumpkin with single bow

- Dried florals, such as autumn leaves, wheat, and bittersweet
- Hot glue gun
- 18" (46 cm) of 24-gauge wire
- Miscellaneous items: dish soap, scrub brush, paper towels, newspaper, ruler, scissors

1 *Preparation:* Let pumpkins soak in a sink of warm water, if extremely dirty. Use dish soap and scrub brush to wash them off completely. Use paper towels to dry, and let dry overnight before painting.

2 *Solid Gold & Copper Pumpkins:* Set up newspaper sheets outdoors or in a well-ventilated area. Follow the manufacturer's instructions to spray the pumpkins with a thin coat of paint. Do not attempt to cover the entire pumpkin. Wait at least 15 minutes, or manufacturer's recommended waiting time, between coats, and apply another thin coat of paint. Continue to apply several thin coats of paint, until satisfied with coverage. Be sure to use several thin coats rather than 1 or 2 thick coats, because spray paint runs and globs if applied too thick.

3 *Multicolored Pumpkin:* Set up newspaper sheets outdoors or in a well-ventilated area. Follow the manufacturer's instructions to spray the pumpkin with a thin coat of gold. Do not attempt to cover the entire pumpkin. Wait at least 15 minutes, or manufacturer's recommended waiting time, between coats, and apply another thin coat of copper. See the Step 3 illustration to continue to apply several thin coats of a different color paint each time, until desired look is obtained.

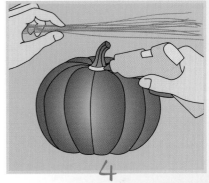

4 *Dried Florals:* Repeat Step 2 or 3 to paint the dried florals, although not as many coats will be needed. Let dry. Refer to the photo and the Step 4 illustration to hot-glue dried florals to the top of pumpkin.

5 *Bows:* For the solid gold and copper pumpkins make a 10-loop, 9" (23 cm) diameter bow with 8" (20.5 cm) streamers. Twist 6" (15 cm) of 24-gauge wire around the center of the ribbon; twist tightly to secure. See the Step 5 illustration to twist the wire ends around the pumpkin stem; trim ends short or tuck in under the ribbon. For the single bow on the multicolored pumpkin, tie the ribbon onto the pumpkin stem, and make a bow. For all pumpkins, make sure to cover the dried floral stem ends with the ribbon and bows.

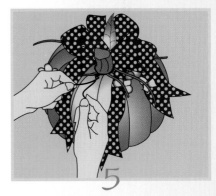

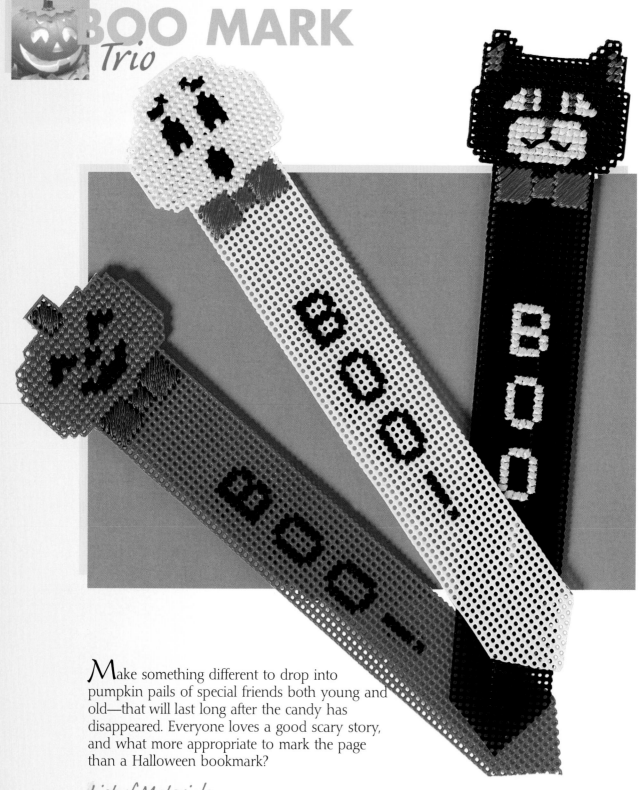

Make something different to drop into pumpkin pails of special friends both young and old—that will last long after the candy has disappeared. Everyone loves a good scary story, and what more appropriate to mark the page than a Halloween bookmark?

List of Materials

- 1 sheet each 14-count perforated plastic: orange for the pumpkin, white for the ghost, black for the cat
- Ribbon floss or 6-strand embroidery floss: 6 yd. (5.5 m) black, 4 yd. (3.7 m) white, 4 yd. (3.7 m) orange, 2 yd. (1.85 m) green
- No. 24 tapestry needle
- Scissors

Boo Mark Trio Color Key

Symbol	Stitch
●	Black Full Cross-Stitch
○	White Full Cross-Stitch
▲	Orange Full Cross-Stitch
■	Green Full Cross-Stitch
✔	Black Half Cross-Stitch
✔	White Half Cross-Stitch
⊘	Orange Half Cross-Stitch
∫	Green Slanting Gobelin
╱	Orange Slanting Gobelin
—	Black Backstitches

1 *Preparation:* Refer to the Plastic Canvas General Instructions and Stitches on page 159. Use scissors to cut three 22x100-hole pieces of perforated plastic. Follow the bold outline on the Stitch Charts to cut out desired bookmark shape from perforated plastic piece with scissors or craft knife.

2 *Charts:* Each square on the Stitch Chart represents one 4-hole square of perforated plastic. Symbols correspond to the colors on the Color Key. Use 1 strand of ribbon floss or 6 strands of embroidery floss to stitch the design.

3 *Stitching:* Work the neckties and jack-o'-lantern stem with Slanting Gobelin stitches. Work BOO! in full cross-stitches. Work the jack-o'-lantern eyes, nose and mouth; ghost eyes, eyebrows and mouth; and cat eyes and muzzle in full cross-stitches. Fill in the jack-o'-lantern and ghost face backgrounds in half cross-stitches. Fill in the cat face background and ears in half cross-stitches. Backstitch the muzzle lines on the cat with black.

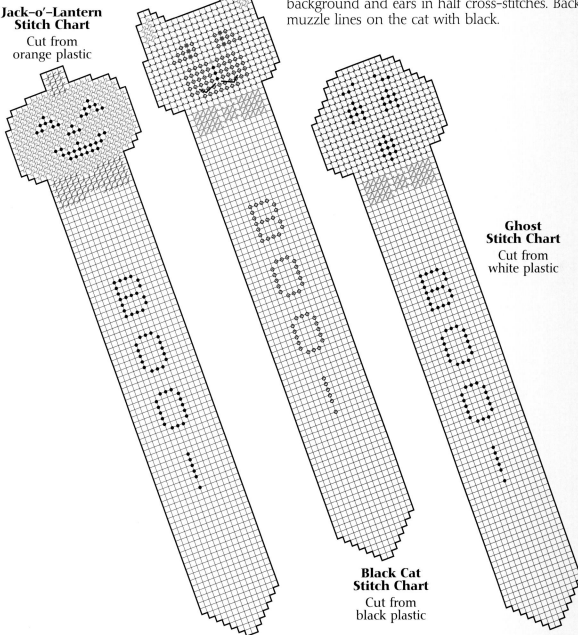

Jack–o'–Lantern Stitch Chart
Cut from orange plastic

Ghost Stitch Chart
Cut from white plastic

Black Cat Stitch Chart
Cut from black plastic

WHAT'S COOKIN'
Apron

Whether you're passing treats out at school or at the front door, you'll want to dress for the occasion. Greet trick-or-treating goblins, witches and monsters dressed in a not-too-scary apron with pockets full of party favors!

List of Materials

- Premade natural canvas apron

- Cotton fabrics for appliqués: 6" x 10" (15 x 25.5 cm) gray, 4" x 8" (10 x 20.5 cm) black, 7" x 9" (18 x 23 cm) Halloween print, two 4" (10 cm) squares coordinating mini-prints

- 9" x 22" (23 x 56 cm) Halloween print fabric for pockets

- Six 4" (10 cm) muslin squares

- ¼ yd. (0.25 m) fusible web

- Fabric paints: brown, light green, dark green, peach, orange, white

- Fabric paintbrushes: small flat, liner

- Pattern Sheet

- Miscellaneous items: iron, tracing paper, pencil, scissors, masking tape, air-soluble marker, zigzag sewing machine and black thread, black fine-point permanent-ink marker, straight pins, ruler

1 *Appliqués:* Wash, dry and press apron and fabrics; do not use fabric softener. Follow manufacturer's instructions to iron fusible web to wrong side of cotton appliqué fabrics. Trace 7 individual appliqué patterns to tracing paper, and cut out. Follow the dotted lines to add extra fabric for underlap on the front and neck of the dress and the top of the hair. Reverse patterns, trace onto paper side of appropriate fused fabric, and cut out.

2 *Witch & Cauldron:* Trace entire pattern to tracing paper. Center pattern under upper apron bib, and secure with masking tape. Tape apron up to a window or hold over a light source, and trace pattern to front of apron with air-soluble marker as shown in the Step 2 illustration. Remove tape, lay apron flat and place appliqués on in the following order, and fuse 1 at a time: dress, hair, hat and cauldron.

3 *Appliquéing:* Set the sewing machine for a closely spaced, medium-width zigzag or satin stitch. Loosen the needle thread tension, if necessary, so bobbin thread won't show on the right side of the fabric. Stitch with black thread so the zigzag is halfway between the appliqué piece and the apron. Stitch the hat and cauldron each in a continuous line, then the hair, and complete the dress.

4 *Painting:* Refer to the photo and Step 4 illustration and use the fabric brush to paint: witch's face and hands with peach, the frog light green with dark green spots, stirring stick with brown, words with orange, cauldron and frog eyes with white/green, question mark with white. Use black marker to outline all, and add eyes and mouth to witch.

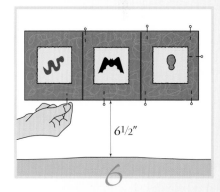

5 *Pocket:* Press edges of pocket Halloween print fabric under 1/4" (6 mm) twice; stitch a hem 1/8" (3 mm) all around. Align and stack muslin squares in pairs. Center and pin pairs, evenly spaced, on pocket fabric. Follow the Step 3 instructions to satin-stitch around edges of muslin squares.

6 *Pocket Appliqués:* Fuse snake, bat and spider centered in the muslin squares. Follow the Step 3 instructions to satin-stitch around appliqué edges. Pin pocket on apron 6½" (16.3 cm) from bottom; topstitch around bottom and side edges. Mark vertical lines centered between the muslin squares with air-soluble marker, as shown in the Step 6 illustration. Pin, and stitch along lines between squares to form 3 pockets.

7 *Finishing:* Refer to the photo and use black marker to write "Snake Tongues," "Bat Wings" and "Spider Legs." Also draw in spider legs and snake tongue. Use liner brush handle to dot eyes with white paint, then green. Paint bat mouth white.

HALLOWEEN
Earrings

Halloween earrings in many designs are for your choosing; make them either out of shrink plastic or modeling clay.

List of Materials

For Clay Pumpkin Earrings

- 1 pkg. 50 g orange oven-bake modeling clay
- Industrial-grade or jewelry adhesive
- ⅛ yd. (0.15 m) green satin ribbon, 1/16″ (1.5 mm) wide
- 1 pair earring backs

For Shrink Plastic Earrings

- 8½″ x 11″ (21.8 x 28 cm) clear shrink plastic
- Soft-lead colored pencils: white, black, light green, orange, yellow, peach, pink, dark green
- Jewelry findings: 3 pairs of ear wires, four 5 mm jump rings

- Pattern Page 169
- Miscellaneous items: kitchen knife, nonstick baking sheet, black extra-fine-point permanent-ink marker, fine sandpaper, scissors, ⅛″ (3 mm) hole punch, needlenose pliers

Clay Pumpkin Earrings

1 *Preparation:* Divide clay into 8 pieces. Follow manufacturer's instructions to knead each piece until it feels warms, like smooth putty. Roll clay between palms to make a pumpkin shape. Cut pumpkin in half with kitchen knife.

2 *Baking:* Use the kitchen knife to score lines in the pumpkin. Make a small indentation with thumb for the stem on pumpkin top. Bake according to clay manufacturer's instructions, usually 20-30 minutes until hardened on a baking sheet in a 265°F (132°C) oven.

3 *Decorating:* Refer to the photo and the illustration to draw jack-o'-lantern face on clay pumpkin with black marker. Cut green satin ribbon in half; make a knot in the center of each piece. Use adhesive to glue ribbon stems on top, and earring backs on the back of each pumpkin.

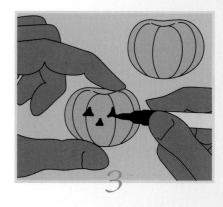

Shrink Plastic Earrings

1 *Preparation:* Follow manufacturer's instructions on how to use shrink plastic. Evenly sand the wrong side of the plastic; be careful to sand everywhere, as pencil colors will not adhere to unsanded surfaces. Note that plastic may have a grain and shrink more in 1 direction than the other. Place plastic, sanded side down, over earring pattern; trace all lines with black marker.

2 *Coloring:* Use the colored pencils to color the designs, referring to the photo and the Step 2 illustration:

Ghost: Body white, and eyes black.

Witch: Hat and gown black. Gown lines and hat lining light green. Jack-o'-lantern, hat band and sleeve lining orange. Jack-o'-lantern eyes and nose yellow. Face and hands peach. Cheeks pink. Eyes dark green.

Jack-o'-Lantern: Pumpkins orange. Eyes black. Nose and mouth yellow. Leaves light green with dark green veins.

3 *Baking:* Carefully cut out all pieces with scissors. Use paper punch to punch holes as indicated on the pattern. Bake and cool according to shrink plastic manufacturer's instructions.

4 *Finishing:* Use needlenose pliers to attach ear wires to the top of each earring. Insert the jump rings to attach leaves between the big and little jack-o'-lanterns, as shown in the Step 4 illustration. Pinch rings closed with needlenose pliers.

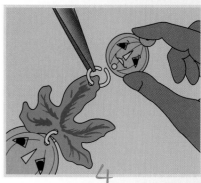

$\mathcal{T}$his year, leave the moaning and groaning to the ghosts, because there's no trick to this quick project. Fabric leftovers make this stuffed spooky scene in a frightful flash.

List of Materials

- Cotton fabrics: 4″ x 8″ (10 x 20.5 cm) yellow, 7″ x 12″ (18 x 30.5 cm) white, 6″ x 10″ (15 x 25.5 cm) black, 8″ (20.5 cm) square orange pin-dot, 1″ x 2″ (2.5 x 5 cm) green/beige plaid
- Embroidery floss: black, gray, orange, green
- Polyester fiberfill
- 1/3 yd. (0.32 m) orange picot satin ribbon, 1/4″ (6 mm) wide
- 6 jumbo wood craft sticks
- Antique white acrylic paint and 1″ (2.5 cm) sponge brush
- Wire: 24″ (61 cm) of 20-gauge craft, 1 yd. (0.95 m) green cloth-covered floral
- Five 1″ (2.5 cm) green silk leaves
- Hot glue gun
- Pattern Sheet
- Miscellaneous items: tracing paper, pencil, scissors, pinking shears, ruler, drill with 1/16″ bit, wire cutters, embroidery needle, 3″ (7.5 cm) square cardboard

1 *Cutting:* Trace 7 patterns to tracing paper, and cut out; use pinking shears to cut out ghost and cat. Also cut two 1/4″ (6 mm) black circles for ghost eyes.

2 *Fence:* Lay 4 wood craft sticks vertically 3/4″ (2 cm) apart for posts, as shown in the Step 2 illustration. Glue 2 remaining sticks horizontally across posts. Drill hole in each outer fence post top. Thin antique white paint with water and use sponge brush to paint fence; let dry.

3 *Hanger:* Loosely curl craft wire around finger. Refer to the photo and thread wire ends through outer fence holes; twist to secure.

4 *Figure Assembly:* Refer to Embroidery Stitches on page 158. Place fabric wrong sides together and use 3 strands of black floss to sew running stitches 1/4″ (6 mm) from edge. Leave small opening for fiberfill as shown in the Step 4 illustration. Stuff lightly and continue sewing to close. Glue eyes to ghost and tie orange ribbon bow.

5 *Cat:* Satin-stitch small nose with 3 strands of gray floss. Insert needle on side of nose for whiskers, and come up on other side. Trim floss, leaving 1/2″ (1.3 cm) ends on each side. Repeat 2 times and trim. Make French knots for eyes.

6 *Pumpkin:* Hot-glue pumpkin base to center of wrong side of orange pin-dot pumpkin fabric. Use 3 strands of orange floss to sew gathering stitches along fabric edge. Gather fabric to form a cup; stuff. Pull thread tight and knot. Hot-glue on pumpkin face. Use 3 strands of green floss to sew stem pieces, wrong sides together, with small running stitches. Hot-glue to center top.

7 *Vines:* Cut one 18″ (46 cm), one 9″ (23 cm), one 7″ (18 cm) and one 2″ (5 cm) piece of floral wire. Curl wires around pencil for tight curls and finger for loose curls. Refer to the photo and the Step 7 illustration to wrap 3 long wires for vines around lower left fence corner; hot-glue to fence back to secure. Hot-glue short wire to pumpkin stem and leaves to vines.

8 *Scene Assembly:* Refer to photo to hot-glue ghost, cat, moon and pumpkin to fence; pumpkin is freestanding.

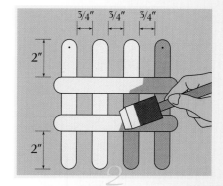

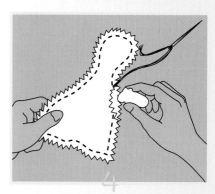

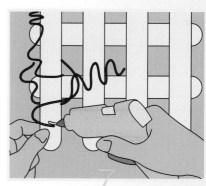

$\mathcal{I}$t is said, everything you need to know you learned in kindergarten, and that is very true with this bountiful autumn tray. It's simply done by coloring in a pattern with oil pencils.

List of Materials

- 9″ x 12″ (23 x 30.5 cm) wooden tray with 2″ (5 cm) border*
- Oil pencils in colors listed in Color Key*
- Graphite transfer paper*
- Clear acrylic spray
- Pattern Sheet

- Miscellaneous items: very fine sandpaper, tack cloth, tracing paper, ruler, pencil, red pencil, scissors, masking tape, eraser, pencil sharpener, large makeup brush or paintbrush

*(See Sources on pg. 175 for purchasing information.)

1 *Preparation:* Lightly sand tray front with grain until smooth; remove sanding dust with tack cloth. Trace pattern onto tracing paper, and cut out. Cut apart into a border pattern and a tray pattern.

2 *Transferring:* Cut graphite paper to fit tray pattern, place on tray recessed area, graphite side down. Use masking tape to secure pattern. Trace over the pattern main design lines, not any shading or detail lines, as lightly as possible. See the Step 2 illustration; red pencil shows what has already been traced. Check to see that lines aren't too dark, and that you aren't making grooves in the wood. Remove tape, pattern and graphite. Repeat to transfer corn husks and gourds on border pattern to tray rim. Join any lines freehand that are not continuous between the tray and rim.

3 *Oil Pencils:* These colored pencils blend together smoothly and subtly; practice on 100% cotton drawing paper, some scrap wood or on the back side of the tray before you begin. Use a medium pressure and back-and-forth strokes; sharpen pencils as needed. Don't touch what you have already colored, because it will smear. Place a sheet of paper over colored areas, or try to color left to right (vice versa, if left-handed) or from top to bottom. Whisk away any pencil crumbs with large brush.

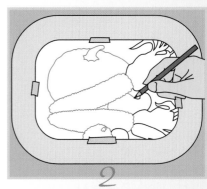

2

4 *Basecoating:* Erase any lines that are too dark before you begin. Lightly color in the vegetables on the tray and border with the colors listed in the Color Key; see the Step 4 illustration.

5 *Details:* Carefully retape graphite paper and tray pattern over colored vegetables, being careful not to smear. Lightly trace detail lines, such as gourd stripes, corn kernels, corn husks, and pumpkin and gourd grooves. Remove tape, pattern and graphite. Repeat with border pattern to trace detail lines on corn husks and gourds. If you would prefer, shade and do details freehand. Join any lines freehand that are not continuous between the tray and rim. Follow the Color Key and see the Step 5 illustration to outline, shade, highlight and do all the vegetable details in the order listed.

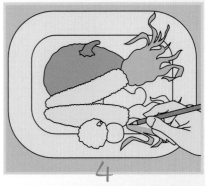

4

6 *Border:* Repeat Step 2 to transfer diamonds on border pattern to tray rim. Carefully outline each diamond with black; fill in the remainder of the border with black. Turn the tray as you work to prevent smudging. Because this is such a large area to color, you could also use black acrylic craft paint, and paint the border, masking off the diamonds with masking tape.

7 *Finishing:* Lightly spray the entire tray with a few light coats of acrylic sealer, following manufacturer's instructions. If you want more protection, apply a brush-on waterbase varnish to the front, back and edges after applying 1 coat of spray sealer; the sealer will prevent the varnish from moving any of the colors.

5

This sampler, mounted in a rustic frame, has a simple message that reminds us of why we gather for a feast on Thanksgiving Day. It will also provide a daily reminder to do that which we often forget.

List of Materials

- 12" square (30.5 cm) 14-count khaki Aida cloth
- 1 skein each 6-strand embroidery floss in colors listed on Color Key
- No. 24 tapestry needle
- Mat and frame of your choice
- Miscellaneous items: scissors, iron

1 Preparation: Refer to the Cross-Stitch General Instructions and Stitches on page 158 and the Stitch Charts to cross-stitch the design using 2 strands of floss. Each square on the Chart represents 1 square of Aida cloth. Symbols correspond to the colors on the Color Key.

2 Initials and Date: Choose the letters for your initials from the alphabet at the top of the Sampler Stitch Chart. Draw them in the lower left corner of the chart, beginning in the corner where marked, and stitch accordingly. Stitch the year in the lower right corner using the Date Stitch Chart. Work backward so the right edge of the rightmost number is even with the rightmost row of stitching in the sampler above.

3 Finishing: When stitching is complete, follow the Step 6 instructions on page 158 to launder and press. Mat and frame as desired.

Date Stitch Chart

Give Thanks Sampler Color Key

Symbol	DMC #	Color
o	301	Med. Mohogany
u	400	Dk. Mohogany
×	3012	Med. Khaki Green
■	3021	Vy. Dk. Brown Grey

Give Thanks Sampler Stitch Chart

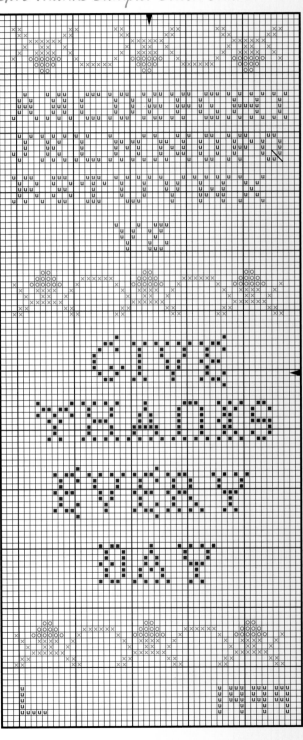

Leaves stenciled in the rich, warm hues of the season skitter across a machine-quilted placemat of green and gold, while a solitary stuffed leaf atop a painted gold wreath enfolds a matching napkin.

List of Materials

For Each Placemat, Napkin & Ring

- 45″ (115 cm) cotton fabrics: ½ yd. (0.5 m) each of olive green and gold

- Leaf stencils, different sizes

- Acrylic craft paints: burgundy, green, burnt orange, russet, gold metallic

- Paintbrushes: five ⅝″ (1.5 cm) stencil, No. 8 round

- 13″ x 17″ (33 x 43 cm) cotton batting

- 1¾ yd. (1.6 m) green piping, ³/₁₆″ (4.5 mm) wide

- 1″ (2.5 cm) masking tape

- 3¼″ (8.2 cm) vine wreath

- Polyester fiberfill, small amount

- Miscellaneous items: yardstick, scissors, disappearing-ink marker, straight pins, bowl, sewing machine with matching threads, iron, paint palette, soft cloth, pinking shears, white craft glue

1 *Preparation:* Cut a 9½" x 13" (24.3 x 33 cm) rectangle from the olive green fabric. Cut 4½" x 9½" (11.5 x 24.3 cm) and 4½" x 16½" (11.5 x 41.8 cm) rectangles from the gold fabric. Stitch all pieces right sides together with ½" (1.3 cm) seam allowances. Press seams open.

2 *Stitching:* Pin the smaller gold rectangle to the green rectangle, matching raw edges, along the 9½" (24.3 cm) edge. See the Step 2A illustration, and stitch. Pin the remaining gold rectangle to the top of the green/gold piece, and stitch. Place a bowl or saucer in each corner, and trace around with marker; see 2B. Cut along traced lines for rounded corners.

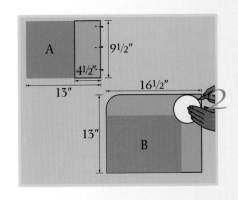

3 *Stenciling:* Use the Dry-Brushing Technique on page 161 for stenciling; let paint dry between each color. Refer to the photo to stencil overlapping leaves randomly around the gold fabric with acrylic paints. Apply paint in a circular motion around the leaf edges. Occasionally overlap onto the green fabric, but leave ¼" (6 mm) around gold fabric outer edge.

4 *Backing and Batting:* Use the painted placemat as a pattern, and trace onto the batting and green fabric for the backing; cut out. Layer placemat top facedown, and batting; pin and baste around.

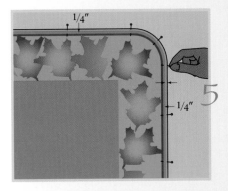

5 *Piping:* Begin in any corner to pin piping to the right side of the placemat top, matching raw edges and with a ¼" (6 mm) seam allowance; see the Step 5 illustration. Stitch, using the zipper foot; overlap the ends. Pin the placemat to the backing, placemat top down, and stitch as close as possible to the piping. Leave a 3" (7.5 cm) opening on 1 long side for turning. Turn right side out; slipstitch the opening closed.

6 *Quilting:* Machine-quilt, stitching in the ditch with green thread along the seamlines between the gold and green fabric. Place masking tape as shown in the Step 6 illustration to make guides for 5 each horizontal and vertical quilting lines.

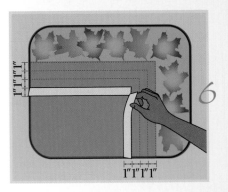

7 *Napkin:* Cut an 18" (46 cm) square from the gold fabric. Turn the edges under ¼" (6 mm) twice, and press. Refer to the photo to stitch around the napkin close to the edge, and then ¼" (6 mm) from the first stitching line.

8 *Napkin Ring:* Mix 1 part russet paint with 1 part water. Use the round brush to paint the wreath quickly with the mixture, covering all the crevices. Wipe up any excess with soft cloth. Dry-brush gold paint on wreath top.

9 *Stuffed Leaf:* Stencil a small burgundy leaf onto green fabric. Let dry, and cut out around stencil, leaving at least ½" (1.3 cm) around edges. Pin another piece of green fabric under the stenciled leaf. Stitch together ⅛" (3 mm) outside the stenciled edges with green thread. Use the pinking shears to cut out the leaf ¼" (6 mm) away from the stenciled edges. Fray the fabric edges with your fingers. Cut a small slit in the leaf back; stuff with fiberfill, and slipstitch closed. Glue the leaf onto the napkin ring. Fold and insert the napkin through the ring.

COPPER
Candle Holders

For autumn entertaining and family gatherings, these shimmering copper cylinders will add a festive touch to your tabletop. Use the leaf patterns provided or gather your own leaves to personalize.

List of Materials

For Each Candle Holder & Base

- 12" square (30.5 cm) mediumweight copper sheet
- Black steel-tipped pen or marker

- Drill and ¹¹/₆₄" bit
- Liquid black shoe polish with sponge applicator
- 11 each brass screws and nuts, ⁴/₄₀" (2.5 mm) diameter, ¹/₄" (6 mm) length for screws
- Pattern Page 174

- Miscellaneous items: marker, ruler, scissors, tracing paper, pencil, masking tape, cardboard or cutting mat, craft knife, hammer, soft cloth, carbon paper, flat screwdriver or dull pencil

136

1 *Preparation:* Mark on the copper sheet: a 6″ x 12″ (15 x 30.5 cm) rectangle, and two 6″ (15 cm) squares. Use scissors to cut out. Trace desired leaf pattern to tracing paper, and cut out.

2 *Base Bottom:* Tape a copper square to cardboard or cutting mat. See the Step 2 illustration to mark 1⅛″ (2.8 cm) margins and 8 drill holes with the black steel-tipped pen. Place a ruler along the foldlines, and score lightly with a craft knife. Make a cut on each edge up to the foldline as shown. Drill holes from the front.

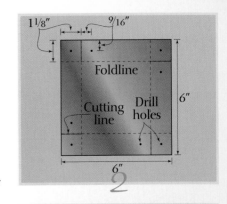

3 *Distressing & Assembly:* Pound on the base with a hammer to distress it. Rub on black shoe polish; use a soft cloth to wipe off excess. Repeat until satisfied. Gently fold edges down along the scored foldline and drilled corner squares. Align drilled holes in each corner, put a screw in each hole, and fasten inside with a nut.

4 *Base Top:* Tape remaining copper square to cardboard. See the Step 4 illustration to make: a center mark on each edge, the 4¼″ (10.8 cm) square within, and a 6″ (15 cm) diameter circle. Cut out the circle with scissors. Mark 4 holes as shown, and drill from front. Place a ruler along the foldlines, and score lightly with a craft knife.

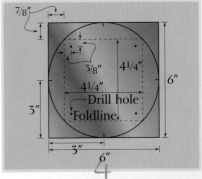

5 *Top Assembly:* Distress and antique top; gently fold circular edges down, distressed side facing out. Place base top on base bottom as shown in the photo; use pen to mark through drilled holes in base top onto base bottom. Drill holes; place the base top on the base bottom. Align drilled holes; put a screw in each hole from the top and fasten with a nut from beneath the base.

6 *Holder:* Tape copper rectangle to cardboard. See the Step 6 illustration to measure and mark: 6 drill holes and margins along the short edges, three 3⅝″ (9.3 cm) rectangles and 1¼″ (3.2 cm) wide and ¾″ (2 cm) long triangles if you desire the scalloped edge. Drill holes from front and cut out scallop triangles. Layer carbon paper, then leaf pattern over center rectangle; trace onto carbon using black marker. Trace onto 2 side rectangles; leaves will touch. Remove pattern and carbon paper.

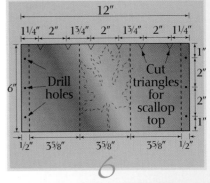

7 *Embossing:* Firmly retrace leaf and veins with pen, transferring image to back side. Turn copper to back side. Use dull pencil or flat screwdriver to "color" inside the leaf, embossing the front surface and adding a 3-dimensional look; see the Step 7 illustration. Work the copper on both the front and back sides; when you are satisfied, use the pen to outline the leaf and the veins from the front side.

8 *Holder Assembly:* Antique the candle holder, placing most color along the outlines and veins; **do not distress.** Gently bend the copper, overlapping the margins and matching up the drill holes. Put a screw in each hole from the outside; fasten with a nut.

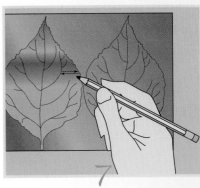

137

CORNUCOPIA
centerpiece

For the Thanksgiving feast, a cornucopia is a traditional centerpiece. However, with preserved roses, autumn leaves and realistic latex fruit instead of Indian corn and gourds, this is a contemporary take on an old classic.

List of Materials

- Wicker cornucopia
- 3" x 4" x 8" (7.5 x 10 x 20.5 cm) dry floral foam
- Sheet moss
- Dried or preserved naturals: 1 spray of autumn leaves, 15-20 nigella pods, 3-4 dozen

miniature red roses, small bunch each of wheat stems and golden yarrow

- Artificial or latex fruit: 4 pomegranates, 3 apples, 2 or 3 grape clusters
- 8 floral picks

- U-shaped floral pins
- 20-gauge wire
- Miscellaneous items: serrated knife, ruler, wire cutters, scrap of paper, awl or ice pick, hot glue gun

1 *Preparation:* Use the serrated knife to cut the floral foam block to fit into the cornucopia, with the top edge of the block about even with the cornucopia edge (see the Step 1B illustration). See 1A to insert 16″ (40.5 cm) of wire in a U-shape through the bottom of the basket into the foam and all the way through. Place a small piece of folded paper or cardboard on top of the foam between the wire ends; see 1B. Twist the wire ends tightly over the paper; this prevents the wire from tearing the foam.

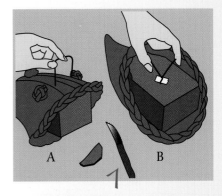

2 *Leaves & Pods:* Cover the foam loosely with sheet moss, and secure with floral pins. Refer to the photo throughout for all arranging steps below. Insert the stems of the autumn leaves into the foam in 1 corner near the bottom, so leaves rest on the table. Insert the nigella pods, 1 stem at a time, arranging them in a bunch next to the leaves.

3 *Grapes:* Refer to the Step 3 illustration to insert the grape clusters on the upper part of the foam, above the leaves. Arrange them so the clusters leave the corner of the foam exposed. If the clusters are short, and the rightmost doesn't reach down over the pods, cut part of 1 cluster off and insert it lower on the foam.

4 *Apples & Pomegranates:* Make a small hole in the base of each fruit with an awl or ice pick. Insert floral pick into the hole; secure with hot glue. Insert the 3 apples as shown in the Step 4 illustration, above the grapes and pods. Insert the 4 pomegranates to the left of the apples, stacking them for dimension, as shown.

5 *Wheat:* See the Step 4 illustration to wrap 6″ (15 cm) of wire around several wheat stems, fastening on a floral pick at the same time. Insert the pick into the exposed foam corner, above the leaves and between the grape clusters.

6 *Roses:* Insert the roses, 1 stem at a time, arranging them in bunches of 15-20, 1 bunch above the wheat between the grape clusters, another above the nigella pods, and a smaller bunch behind the row of fruit along the cornucopia basket edge.

7 *Finishing:* Insert the yarrow stems into the foam, or hot-glue the clusters, in the spaces between and around the apples and pomegranates. Fill in any bare areas with individual leaves or small grape clusters; hot-glue if stems won't reach foam.

TURKEY DAY
Apron

A day of roasting turkey, baking pies and mashing potatoes calls for a special cover-up. Appliquéd with turkeys and pumpkins, this apron is a terrific choice!

140

Thanksgiving Thanksgiving Thanksgiving Thanksgiving Thanksgiving

List of Materials

- Premade natural canvas apron
- 45″ (115 cm) cotton fabrics, ⅛ yd. (0.15 cm) each: 7 coordinating autumn mini-prints, black, light tan, green
- ¼ yd. (0.25 m) fusible web
- ¼ yd. (0.25 m) tear-away fabric stabilizer
- Rust satin ribbon: ½ yd. (0.5 m) ⅛″ (3 mm) wide; ¼ yd. (0.25 m) ⅜″ (1 cm) wide
- ⅛″ (3 mm) black buttons, 20
- Pattern Sheet
- Miscellaneous items: iron, tracing paper, pencil, scissors, ruler, zigzag sewing machine and matching threads, air-soluble marker, hand sewing needle

1 *Preparation:* Wash, dry and press apron and fabrics; do not use fabric softener. Follow manufacturer's instructions to iron fusible web to wrong side of fabrics.

2 *Appliqués:* Trace the 18 individual patterns to tracing paper, and cut out. Trace onto paper side of appropriate fused fabrics, and cut out.

3 *Fusing:* Remove paper backings and refer to the photo to center the large turkey on apron bib front. See the Step 3 illustration to place the appliqués on in the following order, and fuse them in the same order, 1 at a time: feathers, legs, feet, body, head, collar, hat. Refer to photo to place 3 small turkeys with pumpkins in between, evenly spaced, across bottom apron edge. Fuse the small turkeys in the same order as the large turkeys; fuse the pumpkins as follows: back leaf, stem, pumpkin, front leaf.

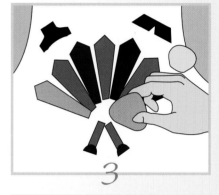

4 *Stabilizer & Hatbands:* Cut a piece of tear-away stabilizer large enough to cover each turkey and pumpkin; baste to apron on wrong side behind corresponding design. Cut 1⅝″ (4 cm) of ⅜″ (1 cm) ribbon for large turkey's hatband; stitch to hat. Cut three ⅞″ (2.2 cm) lengths of ⅛″ (3 mm) ribbon for small turkey hatbands; stitch to hat.

5 *Appliquéing:* Set the sewing machine for a closely spaced, medium-width zigzag or satin stitch. Loosen the needle thread tension, if necessary, so bobbin thread won't show on the right side. Stitch with matching threads so the zigzag is halfway between the appliqué piece and the apron. Stitch turkeys as follows: feather, leg, body, head, feet, hat and collar. See the Step 5 illustration and stitch pumpkins as follows: back leaf, stem, pumpkin and front leaf.

6 *Beak & Eyes:* Refer to pattern and use air-soluble marker to mark beak. Begin at top and satin-stitch beak with orange thread, gradually shortening width of stitches. Tear away stabilizer from apron back and trim loose threads. Refer to photo and the Step 6 illustration to sew buttons for turkey eyes, and 3 buttons down front of each turkey body.

7 *Finishing:* Cut 7″ (18 cm) length of ⅜″ (1 cm) ribbon. Tie bow and tack to large turkey. Cut three 4″ (10 cm) lengths of ⅛″ (3 mm) ribbon. Tie bows and tack to small turkeys.

HANUKKAH SAMPLER
& Table Setting

Keep the lights of Hanukkah permanently lit with a menorah sampler cross-stitched on Aida cloth. The placemat, napkin and bread cover accessories pick up the floral-vine pattern from the bottom of the sampler; they may be used year-round.

List of Materials

For All Projects

- 1 skein each 6-strand embroidery floss and 1 metallic gold thread spool 43.7 yd. (40 m) in colors listed on Color Keys
- No. 24 tapestry needle

For 8″ x 7″ (20.5 x 18 cm) Sampler

- 12″ x 11″ (30.5 x 28 cm) 14-count smoke Aida cloth

For 1 Placemat, Napkin & Breadcover

- 14-count oatmeal prefinished evenweave 13″ x 18″ (33 x 46 cm) placemat, 15″ (38 cm)

square napkin, and 18″ (46 cm) square breadcover*— measurements include fringe

- Pattern Sheet and Page 171
- Miscellaneous items: scissors, ruler, iron

*(See Sources on page 175 for purchasing information.)

1 *Preparation:* Refer to the Cross-Stitch General Instructions and Stitches on page 158, the Stitch Chart on page 171 for the sampler, and the Stitch Charts on the pattern sheet for the placemat, napkin and breadcover. Each square on the Charts represents 1 square of cloth. Symbols correspond to the colors on the Color Key.

2 *Beginning:* For placemat, begin stitching in center of short placemat edge at center of design, 1″ (2.5 cm) in from fabric, not fringe. Arrows on chart indicate center of design. For napkin and breadcover, measure 1½″ (3.8 cm) in and 1″ (2.5 cm) up from lower right corner. Mark with pin for first stitch, indicated by arrow on chart. Work entire chart in 1 corner for breadcover; for napkin, work 9 pattern repeats along edge, work corner motif, and repeat all around. For sampler, follow the instructions in Step 1 on page 158.

3 *Stitching:* Use 2 strands of floss or 1 strand of gold metallic thread to stitch the design. Use 12″ (30.5 cm) strands of the gold metallic thread, rather than the usual 18″ (46 cm) lengths, for less tangles while stitching. Use 1 strand of Dk. Royal Blue No. 796 to backstitch around the bird and 1 strand of gold metallic thread to backstitch around the Hebrew letters. Mount, mat and frame sampler as desired.

ANGEL VESTS
for Mother & Child

Denim or felt vests are easily decorated with cute country Christmas angels and stars that are made of fabric or felt, and then fused on. Finish the appliqué edges with machine stitching or hand embroidery.

List of Materials

For Both Vests

- Vest: adult-size denim or child-size felt
- Paper-backed fusible web: 1 yd. (0.95 m) for adult vest, ¼ yd. (0.25 m) for child's vest
- Pattern Pages 172–173

For Mother's Vest

- 45" (115 cm) cotton fabrics: ¼ yd. (0.25 m) each 6 assorted red and green prints, 4" x 6" (10 x 15 cm) peach, 3" x 8" (7.5 x 20.5 cm) each yellow and brown print

- 2 heart Battenberg doilies, 6" (15 cm) long*
- Red plaid dish towel*
- Flat buttons: 2 black ¼" (6 mm), 4 red ½" (1.3 cm)
- 1¼" (3.2 cm) red ribbon rose
- 1 yd. (0.95 m) tear-away stabilizer

For Child's Vest

- 9" x 12" (23 x 30.5 cm) felt sheets: cranberry, gold, off-white, tan, denim blue

- 1 skein each 6-strand embroidery floss to match felt: denim blue, gold, cranberry
- Miscellaneous items: tracing paper, pencil, ruler, scissors, iron, disappearing-ink pen, straight pins, sewing machine with gold metallic and matching threads, press cloth, embroidery needle, powdered blush, cotton swab

*(See Sources on pg. 175 for purchasing information.)

144

Mother's Vest

1 *Patterns:* Trace the 7 patterns to tracing paper, **adding ¼" (6 mm) all around;** cut out. Trace the number indicated on patterns onto paper back of fusible web; cut out. Follow the manufacturer's instructions to fuse to the wrong side of the fabrics; cut out.

2 *Tree Branches:* Draw the following squares on the paper back of fusible web: three 6½" (16.3 cm), two 5½" (14 cm), one 4½" (11.5 cm), and two 3½" (9 cm), and cut out. Fuse the squares to the wrong side of the 6 assorted red and green fabrics; cut out. Use disappearing-ink pen and ruler to make a diagonal line across each square, and cut to make 16 triangles; see the Step 2 illustration.

3 *Fusing Trees:* Remove paper backing from the appliqués. Lay out for placement, referring to the photo. Remove all but the bottom tree triangle or trunk on the trees, and the angel legs. Fuse trees from the bottom up. Both vest front trees have a trunk and a star; the right tree has 4 triangles, the left has 5. Place vest back trees with the bottom triangle almost on the hem.

4 *Fusing Angel:* Fuse as follows: legs, dress, hand, arm, and star. Cut off 2 lace scallops from the lower left of 1 heart doily. See the Step 4 illustration to place the cut doily under the left doily. Place head, tucking the 2 lace scallops under the chin. Pin the 3 doily pieces, remove head, and fuse doilies. Fuse head over doily wing points and 2 lace scallops.

5 *Appliquéing:* Cut stabilizer to fit each fused design; pin to wrong side of vest. Refer to photo to machine-satin-stitch angel's halo with gold metallic thread. Use white thread to straight-stitch around doily wings. Satin-stitch around the remaining appliqués with matching threads, stitching in fusing order. Tear away the stabilizer. Use matching thread to sew a red button to each star center and black buttons for angel's eyes. Tack ribbon rose under angel's chin.

Child's Vest

1 *Patterns:* Trace the 8 pattern pieces to tracing paper, and cut out. Follow manufacturer's instructions to apply fusible web to the felt sheets. Trace patterns to paper backing as indicated on pattern pieces, and cut out. Remove the paper backing from the appliqués.

2 *Fusing:* Refer to the photo; lay out the appliqués for placement. Place the angel and 1 large tan star on 1 side, and the 3 remaining stars on the other side. Remove all angel pieces except for wings, hands and feet, as shown in the Step 2 illustration. Cover the appliqués with a press cloth, and fuse as follows: wings, hands, feet, sleeves, dress, head and stars.

3 *Embroidery:* Refer to page 158 for Embroidery Stitches. Use 3 strands of floss to work blanket stitches around the appliqué and vest edges. Use gold around the vest, angel dress and sleeves. Use blue around the stars, wings, head, hands and feet. Freehand-draw a smile and 2 eyes on the face with the disappearing-ink pen. Backstitch the mouth with 2 strands of cranberry. Work blue 3-wrap French knots for the eyes. Apply blush to the angel cheeks with cotton swab.

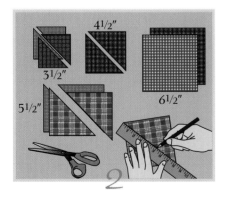

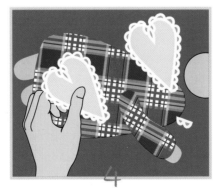

145

BIRDHOUSE Tray

*T*hree snow-topped birdhouses sit quietly under a starry winter sky, surrounded by a gleaming foil finish.

List of Materials

- Wood*: 12" x 16" (30.5 x 40.5 cm) oval tray; three 2¼" to 3" (6 to 7.5 cm) mini birdhouses; five ¾" to 1⅛" (2 to 2.8 cm) stars

- Acrylic paints: tomato, ivory, green, blue, brown, golden brown, metallic gold

- Copper foil and foil adhesive

- Crackle medium
- Textured iridescent snow paint
- Paintbrushes: No. 8 and soft 1" (2.5 cm) flat, three 1" (2.5 cm) sponge
- 7" (18 cm) twigs
- Spanish moss

- Hot glue gun
- Miscellaneous items: sandpaper, tack cloth, paint palette

*(See Sources on pg. 175 for purchasing information.)

1 *Preparation:* Lightly sand the tray and the birdhouses; remove dust with a tack cloth. Refer to Painting Instructions and Techniques on page 160.

2 *Basecoating:* Use the sponge brushes and follow the Painting Guide to basecoat the tray, birdhouses and stars; let dry between colors and coats.

3 *Tray Rim:* Follow manufacturer's instructions to apply an even coat of foil adhesive onto the front and back tray rim. Let the adhesive dry until it is clear or tacky. See the Step 3 illustration and follow the manufacturer's instructions to apply the copper foil with soft brush to the adhesive on both sides of the tray rim. Follow manufacturer's instructions to apply an even coat of crackle medium to the front and back tray rim, brushing in only 1 direction.

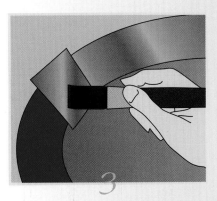

4 *Tray Center:* Apply the crackle medium to the tray center on the front side. When the medium is tacky to the touch, apply an even coat of ivory. Brush in the same direction as how the medium was applied; see the Step 4 illustration. Repeat to crackle the back side of the tray.

5 *Birdhouse Roofs:* Repeat Step 3 to apply foil adhesive, copper foil and crackle medium to the roof of each birdhouse.

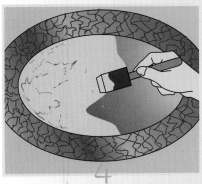

6 *Birdhouses:* Refer to the photo to center and hot-glue the birdhouses to the front of the tray. Arrange and hot-glue the twigs in a bundle below the birdhouses, as shown in the Step 6 illustration. Hot-glue the Spanish moss onto the twigs and in each birdhouse opening.

7 *Finishing:* Use the No. 8 brush to apply the textured snow paint onto the roofs and perches of the birdhouses and the top of the twigs. Refer to the photo to hot-glue the 5 stars to the tray center above the birdhouses.

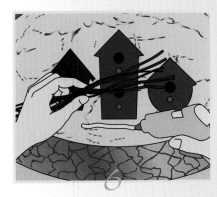

Painting Guide

Tray Rim Front and Back	Tomato
Tray Center Front and Back	Metallic Gold
Birdhouses	Green/Tomato/Blue
Birdhouse Perches	Brown
Stars	Golden Brown

SANTA
Quilt

When your little one (or grown up one!) is anxiously waiting to hear eight tiny reindeer on Christmas Eve, these sixteen Santas will be perfect for snuggling under. With Santa's cheery face smiling from every square, this quilt is a delight to make, whether you hang it on a wall or use it daily to keep warm.

List of Materials

- 45″ (115 cm) cotton/polyester fabrics: ⅞ yd. (0.8 m) green candy cane print, 1⅛ yd. (1.05 m) red print, ⅓ yd. (0.32 m) muslin, 1 yd. (0.95 m) white-on-white print, ⅛ yd. (1.05 m) gold lamé, 2 yd. (1.85 m) royal blue Santa print

- 1 skein light red rayon floss
- Needlepunched cotton batting, 45″ x 60″ (115 x 152.5 cm)
- 32 flat black buttons, ½″ (1.3 cm) wide
- Pattern Page 170

- Miscellaneous items: tracing paper, pencil, scissors, chalk, iron, terry cloth towel, press cloth, sewing machine with matching threads and transparent nylon monofilament, ruler, straight pins, brass safety pins, masking tape, white hand quilting thread

1 *Preparation & Cutting:* Wash, dry and press fabrics. Stitch pieces right sides together using ¼" (6 mm) seams. Press all seams to the darker side. Trace the mustache and eyebrow patterns and cut out as indicated. In addition, cut the items listed in the Cutting Guide on page 170.

2 *Face:* See the Step 2 illustration to fold muslin face in half and pin-mark centers; mark eyes, eyebrows, mustache and nose with chalk. Place mustache on face with raw edges even at the bottom; mark along the dotted stitching lines. Appliqué mustache top and eyebrows, turning under seam allowance. Refer to the Embroidery Stitches on page 158 to satin-stitch the nose using 4 strands of red floss. Press face blocks facedown on soft towel. Use black thread to sew 2 black buttons to each face for the eyes.

3 *Blocks:* See the Step 3 illustration to stitch face blocks in numerical order, 8 with hair on the left side, 8 with hair on the right side and 16 hat side strips. Each Santa block should measure 8½" x 10½" (21.8 x 26.8 cm).

4 *Quilt Top:* See the Step 4A illustration to stitch 2 rows of 4 face blocks, with the hat hanging on the right, and five 10½" (26.8 cm) candy cane strips. Stitch 2 rows of 4 hat-on-the-left face blocks. See 4B to stitch 5 sashing strips from 5 blue Santa print squares and 4 green candy cane strips. Refer to the photo to stitch the Santa face block rows, alternating the right and left hanging hats. Stitch a 35" (89 cm) red print strip to the top and bottom.

5 *Basting:* Cut a blue Santa print backing 2" to 4" (5 to 10 cm) wider than quilt top on each side. Pin-mark side centers of quilt top, backing and batting. Tape backing, right side down, on a flat surface. Begin at the center and work toward corners, stretching slightly. Place batting and quilt top right side up over backing, matching centers. Pin-baste a line up the middle of each side, working from the center outward. Baste each quarter, placing pins about 5" (12.5 cm) apart. Remove tape; fold backing edges over batting and quilt top, and pin.

6 *Quilting:* Machine-quilt in the ditch around each Santa face, hat and block using white thread in the bobbin and monofilament thread in the top, removing the safety pins as needed. Machine-stipple the side hair, mustache and beard with white thread. Quilt an "X" across each blue square with white thread.

7 *Binding:* Stitch 5 binding strips together to form 1 long strip; fold in half lengthwise, wrong sides together. Pin the binding around the quilt top, matching raw edges, and stitch. Turn binding to the back; slipstitch in place.

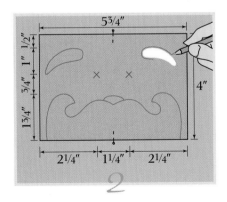

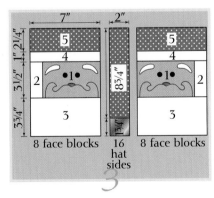

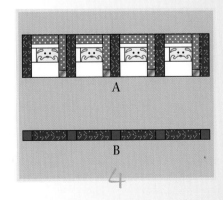

PAPER
Pop-Up Package

$\mathcal{T}$his is the perfect solution to keeping conspicuous gifts like jewelry, candy, cassette tapes or gift certificates under wraps. Best of all, it is environmentally friendly because you can reuse it over and over again.

List of Materials

- Posterboard: 6" x 9" (15 x 23 cm) green, 24" (61 cm) square red
- Star hole paper punch
- Textured or dimensional snow paint
- Glue stick
- Pattern Sheet
- Miscellaneous items: tracing paper, pencil, scissors, ruler, small paintbrush

1 *Preparation:* Trace the 3 patterns to tracing paper, and cut out. Cut out from red and green posterboard as indicated on the patterns. Mark the score lines on box flaps on the back side lightly with pencil and ruler.

2 *Punching:* Lightly mark placement of star holes to be punched on 1 tree with pencil; punch stars where marked as shown in the Step 2 illustration. Place the punched tree over the other 4 unpunched trees, and use as a template to lightly mark dots with pencil for star holes. Punch the remaining 4 trees.

3 *Scoring:* Place flap on flat surface, back side up, with score line at right. See the Step 3 illustration to score lines by holding ruler firmly along line and using back side of scissors blade to lightly mark posterboard. Fold up at score line.

4 *Trees:* Dot each punched tree on the back side with glue stick; be careful not to use too much glue or it will build up and show through the punched star holes. Place the trees on each box flap on the left side, and press into place. Refer to the photo to use paintbrush to apply a line of textured snow along the top of each tree branch. Let both paint and glue dry.

5 *Box Flaps:* See the Step 5 illustration to glue box flaps to wrong side of box base. Match the folded score line with the box base edge, and overlap the corners. Let glue dry.

6 *Closing Box:* Fold flaps toward center, working counterclockwise. Fold tip of fourth flap under first flap. Tuck the entire right edge and tip of last flap under the left edge of the beginning flap.

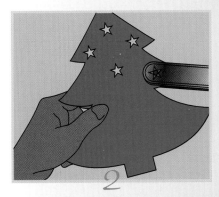

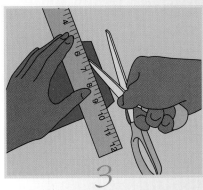

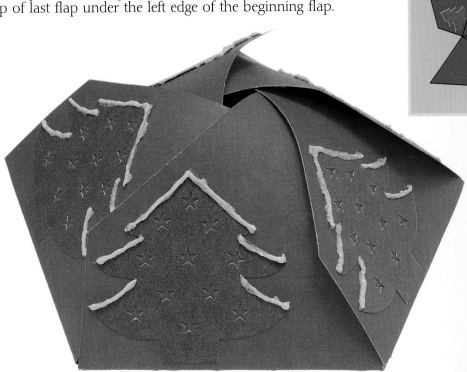

CRAFT STICK
Nativity Ornament

The reason for the season is colorfully portrayed when you paint and glue wooden shapes. Country-look pen-stitch borders and heavenly colors make this ornament one you'll treasure.

List of Materials

- Drill with ³/₃₂″ bit
- Wooden shapes*: 3 jumbo craft sticks; 1 each stars, ⁷/₈″, 1¹/₄″, 1⁵/₈″ (2.2, 3.2, 4 cm); 3 ovals, ⁷/₈″ x 2″ (2.2 x 5 cm); 1 oval, ¹/₂″ x 1¹/₂″ (1.3 x 3.8 cm)
- Acrylic paints: light and medium olive, light and medium blue, tan, medium

and russet brown, ivory, gold, metallic gold
- Paintbrushes: ¹/₄″ (6 mm) stencil, Nos. 3 and 8 round, No. 10/0 liner
- Black fine-point permanent-ink marker
- 10″ (25.5 cm) gold pearl cotton

- Miscellaneous items: scrap wood, tracing and graphite paper, pencil, stylus, paper towels, paint palette, white craft glue, scissors
- Pattern Sheet

*(See Sources on pg. 175 for purchasing information.)

Christmas Christmas Christmas Christmas Christmas Christmas

1 *Preparation:* Place the large star on the scrap wood and drill a hole in 1 point ¼" (6 mm) from the edge. Trace the patterns; use the graphite paper and stylus to transfer the face and head wrap lines to the appropriate ovals.

2 *Basecoating:* Refer to Painting Instructions and Techniques on page 160; let dry between colors and coats. Apply 2 coats of color; use the No. 8 brush to paint the edges and back of 1 shape each with light blue, light olive, ivory and gold. Refer to the Painting Guide and photo to basecoat the 3 stars, 3 craft sticks and 4 oval fronts; use the Nos. 3 and 8 round brushes.

3 *Shading:* Use the stencil brush to dry-brush the edges of the stars, manger and Baby Jesus with metallic gold; Joseph's edges with medium olive; Mary's edges with medium blue; the craft stick edges with russet brown. Refer to the Step 3 illustration.

4 *Details:* Use the liner brush to paint Joseph's hair russet brown and Mary's and Baby Jesus' hair with medium brown. Use the marker to draw stitch lines ⅛" (3 mm) along the edges of all shapes, except the manger oval. Draw stitch lines around the faces, along the head wraps and on the manger oval. Dot the eyes.

5 *Assembly:* Refer to the photo and the Step 5 illustration to glue the ends of the craft sticks together in numerical order to form a triangle for the stable. Glue Baby Jesus to the manger. Glue the manger to the center with Mary and Joseph at each side. Thread pearl cotton through the hole in the large star, and knot the ends. Glue stars on top of each other; glue largest star to the stable top.

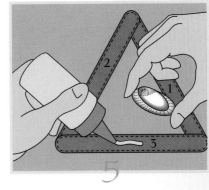

Painting Guide

Stable Craft Sticks	Medium Brown	Joseph's Head Wrap	Light Olive
Stars, Manger	Gold	Joseph's Gown	Medium Olive
Faces	Tan	Baby Jesus' Head Wrap	Metallic Gold
Mary's Head Wrap	Light Blue	Baby Jesus' Gown	Ivory
Mary's Gown	Medium Blue		

This reversible runner has been done in a cheery holly, pinecones and apples Christmas print on one side, and an autumn Thanksgiving harvest print on the other, but any combination of holiday fabrics will work. The key is to find two fabrics that match with the same trim color.

List of Materials

For 14″ x 70″ (35.5 x 178 cm) runner
(Fabric and welting amounts will vary depending on the measurements you get in Step 1 and Step 4)

- 2 yd. (1.85 m) each of 45″ (115 cm) fabric: Christmas print, Thanksgiving print
- 4¾ yd. (4.35 m) red twisted welting, ½″ (1.3 cm) wide

- Miscellaneous items: tape measure, scissors, disappearing-ink marker, ruler, straight pins, transparent tape, sewing machine with matching threads, iron

1 *Measuring for Fabric:* Measure the tabletop length, and add 2 times the desired drop length plus 1" (2.5 cm) for seam allowances. The drop length is how far you want the runner to hang down a side. Decide how wide you want the runner to be, and add 1" (2.5 cm) for seam allowances.

2 *Cutting:* Cut a rectangle the desired length and width from Step 1 from both holiday print fabrics. For 14" x 70" (35.5 x 178 cm) runner shown in photo, cut the fabric 15" x 71" (38 x 180.5 cm).

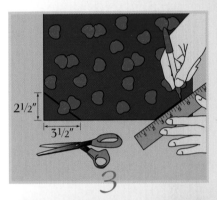

3 *Angling Ends:* Mark 1 end of runner as shown in the Step 3 illustration, 2½" (6.5 cm) from the corner on the long edge, and 3½" (9 cm) from the corner on the short edge. Draw lines diagonally across the corners from marked point to marked point. Cut along the marked lines. Repeat for the other 3 runner ends.

4 *Twisted Welting:* Place 1 runner piece right side up and flat on work surface. Measure all around with a tape measure, including the angled ends. Add 6" (15 cm) extra for joining welting. Pin twisted welting to runner piece, edge of welting tape even with the raw fabric edge. See the Step 4A illustration. Leave 3" (7.5 cm) welting tails; apply transparent tape to both welting ends to prevent fraying. Stitch to runner using zipper foot; leave 1½" (3.8 cm) unstitched between ends.

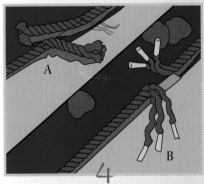

5 *Preparing Welting Ends:* Remove stitching from welting tape on the tails. See the Step 4B illustration. Separate the cords and wrap transparent tape around each end. Trim welting tape to 1" (2.5 cm) from stitching; overlap ends and secure with transparent tape. Arrange cords with right ends up and left ends down.

6 *Joining Welting Ends:* Insert cords at right under welting tape; see 6A. Twist and pull the 3 ends until welting at top is in its original shape. Hold in place with tape or pins. Twist and pull cords at left over cords at right—see 6B—until the top looks like continuous twisted welting; check both sides. Hold ends in place with tape or pins. Place on sewing machine with zipper foot on left side of needle so you stitch in the direction of the twists. Machine-baste through all layers to secure at seamline, or hand-baste, if desired.

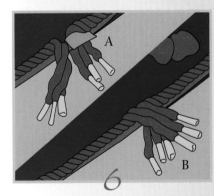

7 *Runner Assembly:* Pin the runner pieces right sides together, matching the raw edges on the long edges. Stitch as close as possible to the welting, using zipper foot, the runner piece with the welting basted on facing down. Leave a 3" (7.5 cm) opening on 1 long side for turning. If desired, flip runner over and stitch again, crowding stitches even closer to welting. Turn right side out, slipstitch the opening closed, and lightly press.

TEACUP
ornaments

If you save too-pretty-to-throw-away teacups with small chips or no saucers, now is the time to get them out of storage. A few ribbon scraps, greenery and beads will give them new life as beautiful ornaments for Christmas.

156

Christmas Christmas Christmas Christmas Christmas Christmas

List of Materials

- Assorted small- to medium-sized china cups (saucers optional)
- Dry floral foam
- Florist clay and pins
- Three 6" (15 cm) squares white tulle
- 10" (25.5 cm) ribbon, assorted colors and widths for bow, 12" (30.5 cm) ribbon or cord for hanger

- Assorted decorations: artificial pine and berries, small pinecones, baby's breath, pearl bead string, small silk roses and leaves, miniature musical instruments, miniature gift packages
- Glues: hot glue gun, epoxy
- Miscellaneous items: serrated knife, wire cutters, fine-gauge wire, scissors

1 *Preparation:* Measure across the depth of each cup. Cut foam with serrated knife to fit, trimming away the bottom to the shape of the cup. Secure the foam to the cup with florist clay. If using a saucer, glue the cup to the saucer with epoxy glue.

2 *Tulle Poufs:* Cut a 6" (15 cm) square of tulle and a 6" (15 cm) length of wire. Gather the 4 corners in 1 hand to make a pouf. Fold the wire in half and poke the ends into the top center of the tulle pouf as shown in 2A. Pull the wire ends down through the corners, so that the tulle looks like a rose; see 2B. Wrap the wires around the gathered corners at the base of the pouf. Make 2 to 3 tulle poufs for each ornament.

3 *Bows:* From ribbon, tie a 3" to 4" (7.5 to 10 cm) double-loop bow; secure the center with 2" (5 cm) of wire and twist the ends together. Poke the wire ends into the foam to attach the bows and tulle poufs to the cup; see the Step 3 illustration. Cut the wire ends short to glue them to the saucer.

4 *Finishing:* Refer to the photo to arrange the decorations in the cup and on the saucer; hot-glue. To hang, insert and glue a florist pin into the foam near the handle. Thread ribbon or cord through the florist pin, and knot the ends together.

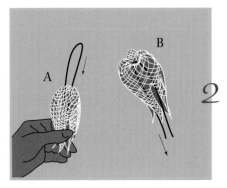

Techniques

EMBROIDERY STITCHES

Backstitch

Up at 1, down at 2, up at 3, down at 1, stitching back to meet previous stitch.

Blanket Stitch

Up at 1, down at 2, up at 3 with thread below needle; pull through.

Blanket Stitch Corner 1

Make a diagonal blanket stitch. Tack stitch at corner, insert needle through loop; pull taut.

Blanket Stitch Corner 2

To work corner, use same center hole to work stitches 1, 2, and 3.

French Knot

Up at 1, wrap thread specified number of times around needle, down near 1.

Running Stitch

Up at odd, down at even numbers for specified length.

Satin Stitch

Up at 1, down at 2, up at 3, working parallel stitches.

CROSS-STITCH

General Instructions

1. Overcast the edges to prevent raveling. Fold the fabric in half vertically and horizontally to find the center, and mark it with a temporary stitch. If desired, place the fabric in an embroidery hoop. Find the center of the design by following arrows on the Chart. Count up and over to the top left stitch or specified point and begin stitching.

2. Each square on a Cross-Stitch Chart represents one square of evenweave fabric, unless otherwise indicated. Symbols correspond to the colors given in the Color Key.

3. Cut floss into 18" (46 cm) lengths. Separate the strands and use the number specified in the project. Stitching tends to twist the floss; allow the needle to hang free from your work to untwist it from time to time.

4. To begin, do not knot the floss, but hold a tail on the back of the work until anchored by the first few stitches. To carry the floss across the back to another area to be stitched, weave the floss under previously worked stitches to new area, but do not carry the floss more than three or four stitches. To end the floss, run it under several stitches on the back, and cut it. Do not use knots.

5. Work all cross-stitches first, then any additional stitches, including backstitches. Work in horizontal rows wherever possible. To make vertical stitches, complete each cross-stitch before moving to the next one.

6. When stitching is completed, wash the fabric in warm sudsy water if needed. Roll it in a terry-cloth towel to remove excess moisture. Press it face-down on another terry-cloth towel to dry.

Aida Stitches

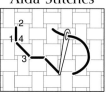

Backstitch

Up at 1, down at 2, up at 3, down at 4, stitching back to meet prior stitch.

Cross-Stitch

Work first half of each stitch left to right; complete each stitch right to left.

Long/Straight Stitch

Work stitches over specified number of threads as indicated on chart.

Linen Stitches

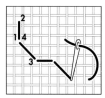

Backstitch

Up at 1, down at 2, up at 3, down at 4, stitching back over two threads to meet prior stitch.

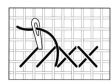

Cross-Stitch

Begin over a vertical thread to work first half of each stitch over two threads, left to right; complete each stitch right to left.

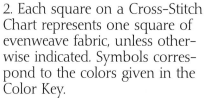

158

PLASTIC CANVAS

General Instructions

1. Each line on a Plastic Canvas Chart represents one bar of plastic canvas.

2. To cut plastic canvas, count the lines on the stitch chart and cut the canvas accordingly, cutting up to, but not into the bordering bars. Follow the bold outlines where given. Use a craft knife to cut small areas.

3. To stitch, do not knot the yarn, but hold a tail in back and anchor with the first few stitches. To end yarn, weave tail under stitches on back; then cut it. Do not stitch over edge bars.

4. When finished stitching individual pieces, finish edges and join pieces as specified with an overcast stitch.

Beaded Half Cross-Stitch

Stitch from lower left, slip on bead, stitch down at upper right over 1 bar of canvas.

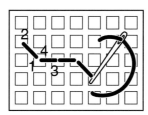

Backstitch

Up at 1, down at 2, up at 3, down at 4, stitching back to meet prior stitch.

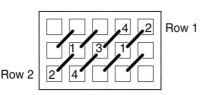

Continental Stitch

Work Row 1, up at 1, down at 2, up at 3, down at 4, working toward left. Work Row 2, up at 1, down at 2, working toward right in established sequence.

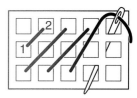

Gobelin Stitch

Up at 1, down at 2, working diagonal stitches over 2 or more bars in direction indicated on graph.

Overcast Stitch

Use a whipping motion over the outer bars to cover or join canvas edges.

PERFORATED PLASTIC

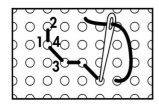

Backstitch

Up at 1, down at 2, up at 3, down at 4, stitching back to meet prior stitch.

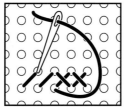

Cross-Stitch

Work first half of each stitch left to right; complete each stitch right to left.

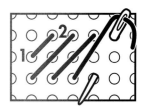

Gobelin Stitch

Up at 1, down at 2, working diagonal stitches in direction indicated on graph.

PAINTING

General Instructions

1. Sanding: Many projects are done on wood, and so must be sanded. If painting on a non-wood surface, make sure it is clean and dry. Begin the process with coarse-grit sandpaper, and end with finer grits. A 150-grit sandpaper will put finish smoothness on surfaces, such as preparing for staining or sanding. A 220-grit extra-fine sandpaper is good for smoothing stained or painted wood before varnishing, or between coats. Use a tack cloth—a treated, sticky cheesecloth—to lightly remove sanding dust after each step. Don't rub over the surface or you will leave a sticky residue on the wood. Wood files, sanding blocks and emery boards can be used to sand hard-to-reach places and curves.

2. Transferring: Place pattern on surface or wood, following direction for grainline. For pattern outlines, such as for cutting your own pieces, use a pencil to trace around pattern piece onto wood. Trace lightly, so wood is not indented. To transfer detail lines, you can use pencil, chalk, transfer paper or graphite paper. Ink beads over many waxed transfer papers, so if you plan to use fine-line permanent-ink markers for detail lines, be sure to use graphite or wax-free transfer paper. Transfer as few lines as possible, painting freehand instead. Do not press hard, or surface may be indented. Use eraser to remove pencil lines, damp cloth on chalk, and paint thinner or soap and water on graphite.

To use pencil or chalk, rub the wrong side of traced pattern. Shake off any loose lead; lay pattern penciled or chalk-side down on wood, and retrace pattern with a pencil or stylus.

To use transfer or graphite paper, place paper facedown on wood, then place pattern on top. Lightly trace over pattern lines. Lay a piece of wax paper on top of pattern to be traced. This protects your original traced pattern and also lets you see what you have traced.

3. Brushes: The size should always correspond in size to the area being painted, preferably with the largest brush that will fit the design area. The brush should also reflect the technique being done, which is usually suggested in craft project directions.

4. Extender: Acrylic extender is a medium to add to acrylic paints to increase their open time. Open time refers to the amount of time in which you can mix and blend the paints before they begin to dry. Those familiar with oil paints are most concerned with this, or if you are doing very complex designs with a great deal of shading.

Comma Strokes

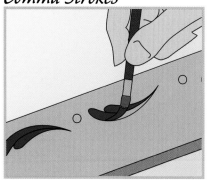

Dots

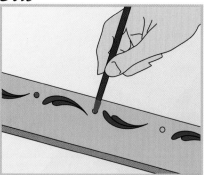

Techniques

Basecoating:
Applying the first coat of paint to a prepared surface, usually covering the surface and all edges in entirety. Sometimes two coats of paint are recommended. Basecoating is usually done with a flat or sponge brush.

Comma Strokes:
This is a stroke that is in the shape of a comma, with a large head and long, curvy thin tail. They come in all shapes and sizes. Begin painting up at the round head and curve down to the tail. Comma strokes require practice before they look right.

Dots:
Dots can be made by dipping the end of the paintbrush or stylus or even a toothpick in paint and then touching it gently on the painted surface. This technique can create perfect eyes or dots better than any brush tip.

160

Double Loading:

This is the same as side loading, except two colors are loaded, one on each side of the brush. The colors gradually blend into one another in the middle of the brush.

Dry-Brushing:

This technique is used to achieve a soft or aged look; many times it is used to blush cheeks. Dip dry brush tips in a small amount of paint (undiluted for heavy coverage and diluted for transparent coverage). Wipe on paper towel until almost no paint is left. Then gently brush on the surface.

Highlighting:

Highlighting is the reverse of shading, causing an area to be more prominent. Thus a lighter color, such as white, is often loaded on a flat brush and used for highlighting. Highlighting is also sometimes done with a liner brush, by painting a straight line with a light color over an area to give a dimensional appearance.

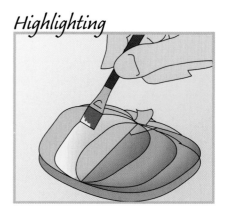

Highlighting

Shading:

Shading is done with a color darker than the main color, making an area recede into the background. It is frequently used on edges of designs and done with the side load or floating technique. On an orange background, the brush is loaded with rust, and pulled along the edge, with the paint edge of brush where color is to be darkest.

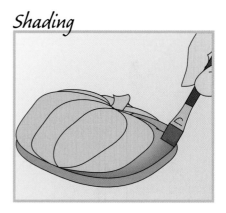

Shading

Side Loading or Floating Color:

Side loading or floating is usually done with a flat or shader brush. Dip or load brush in water; then lightly blot on paper towel to release some moisture. Load or pull one side of the brush through paint. Blend paint on a mixing surface so the color begins to move across the bristles, and is dark on one edge, but light on the other. Make sure to get the paint well blended before actually painting on the surface. Another method is to thin the paint (see below) and mix it well. Load the paint by dipping one corner in and blending well on a mixing surface, as above.

Stippling (or Pouncing):

This is a stenciling technique, and is very similar to dry-brushing, except it gives a more fuzzy or textured look. Stencil, fabric or stippler brushes may be used, or any old scruffy brush. Dip just brush tips in a small amount of paint; then blot on paper towel until brush is almost dry. Apply the paint to the surface by pouncing up and down with the bristle tips until desired coverage is achieved.

Side Loading or Floating Color

Thinning:

Add drops of water and mix until the paint is of an inklike consistency. Sometimes a specific mix of water and paint is requested.

Wash:

Dilute the paint with five parts water to one part paint (or whatever proportion is requested) and mix well. Load the brush, and blot excess paint on brush onto a paper towel. Fill in the area to be painted, giving transparent coverage. A wash can also be used for shading or highlighting large areas.

CROCHET STITCHES

Abbreviations

beg	Beginning
ch	Chain
dc	Double Crochet
lp(s)	Loop(s)
rem	Remaining
rep	Repeat
rnd(s)	Round(s)
sc	Single Crochet
sk	Skip
sl st	Slip Stitch
sp(s)	Space(s)
st(s)	Stitch(es)
tog	Together
yo	Yarn Over
*	Repeat following instructions a given number of times

Beginning Slip Knot

Begin with a slip knot on hook about 6" (15 cm) from end of yarn. Insert hook through loop; pull to tighten.

Chain Stitch (ch)

Yarn over, draw yarn through loop on hook to form new loop.

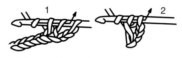

Double Crochet (dc)

1. For first row, yarn over, insert hook into 4th chain from hook. Yarn over; draw through 2 loops on hook.

2. Yarn over, and pull yarn through last 2 loops on hook.

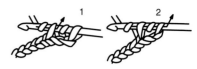

Single Crochet (sc)

1. For first row, insert hook into second chain from hook, and draw up a loop.
2. Yarn over, and draw through both loops on hook.

Slip Stitch (sl st)

Insert hook in stitch, and draw up a loop. Yarn over, and draw through both loops on hook.

Yarn Over (yo)

Wrap yarn over hook from back to front and proceed with specific stitch instructions.

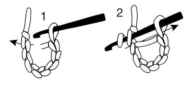

Forming Ring with a Slip Stitch

1. Insert hook in first chain.
2. Yarn over, and pull through all loops on hook.

162

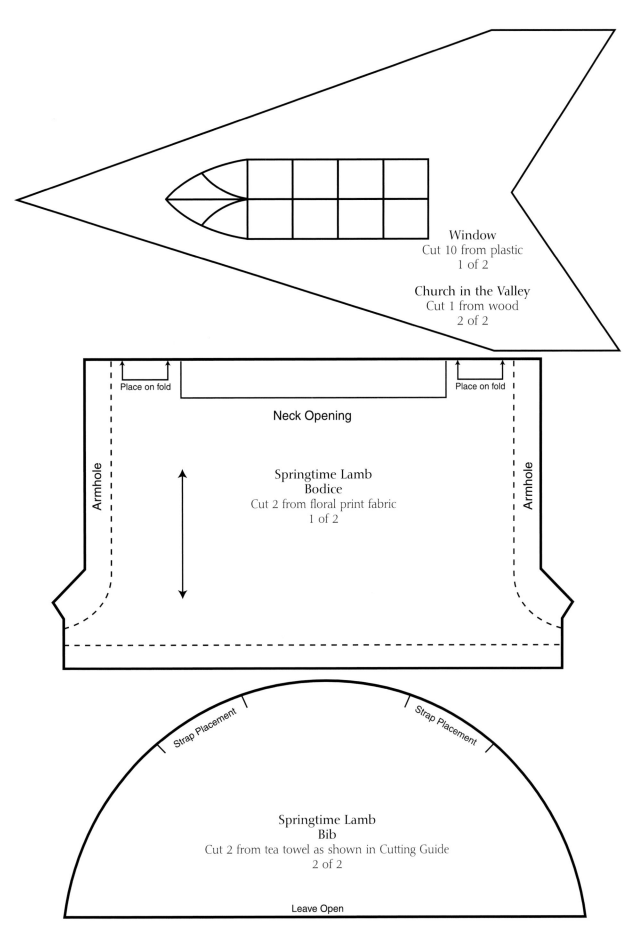

Window
Cut 10 from plastic
1 of 2

Church in the Valley
Cut 1 from wood
2 of 2

Place on fold   Place on fold

Neck Opening

Armhole   Armhole

Springtime Lamb
Bodice
Cut 2 from floral print fabric
1 of 2

Strap Placement   Strap Placement

Springtime Lamb
Bib
Cut 2 from tea towel as shown in Cutting Guide
2 of 2

Leave Open

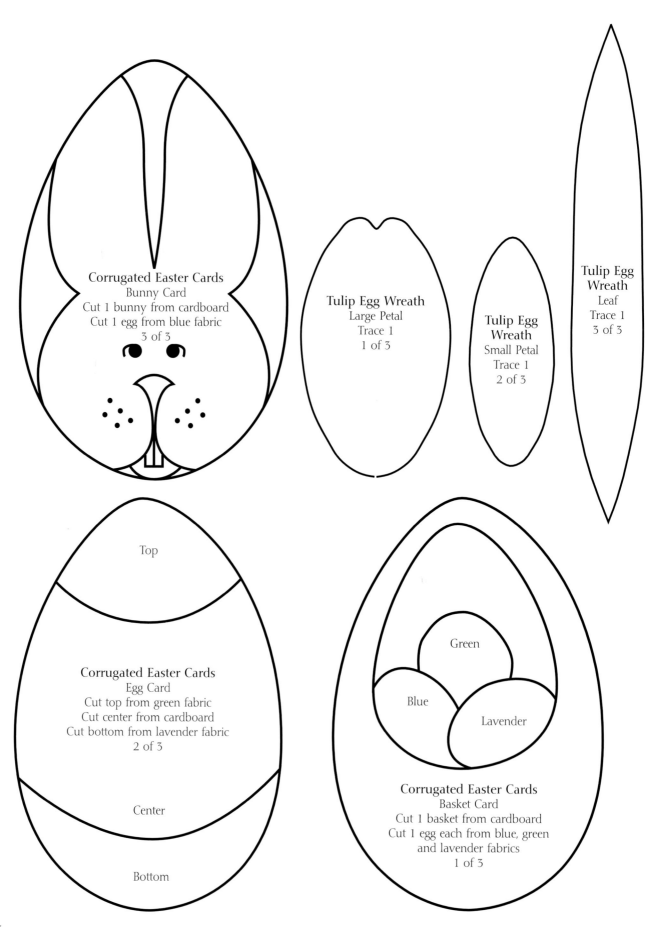

Corrugated Easter Cards
Bunny Card
Cut 1 bunny from cardboard
Cut 1 egg from blue fabric
3 of 3

Tulip Egg Wreath
Large Petal
Trace 1
1 of 3

Tulip Egg
Wreath
Small Petal
Trace 1
2 of 3

Tulip Egg
Wreath
Leaf
Trace 1
3 of 3

Top

Corrugated Easter Cards
Egg Card
Cut top from green fabric
Cut center from cardboard
Cut bottom from lavender fabric
2 of 3

Center

Bottom

Green

Blue

Lavender

Corrugated Easter Cards
Basket Card
Cut 1 basket from cardboard
Cut 1 egg each from blue, green
and lavender fabrics
1 of 3

Heart Smart Pinafore
Half Heart
Cut 1 half heart from fused
cranberry check towel
1 of 3

Cut top half of half heart from
fused navy plaid towel
2 of 3

Cut bottom half of half heart from
fused ecru check towel
3 of 3

Clay Bunny
Body
Trace 1
1 of 6

Clay
Bunny
Arm
2 of 6

Clay
Bunny
Arm
3 of 6

Clay
Bunny
Leg
4 of 6

Clay
Bunny
Leg
5 of 6

Clay
Bunny
Carrot
6 of 6

Nappliqué Bunny Shirt
Bunny
Trace 1 to paper
1 of 1

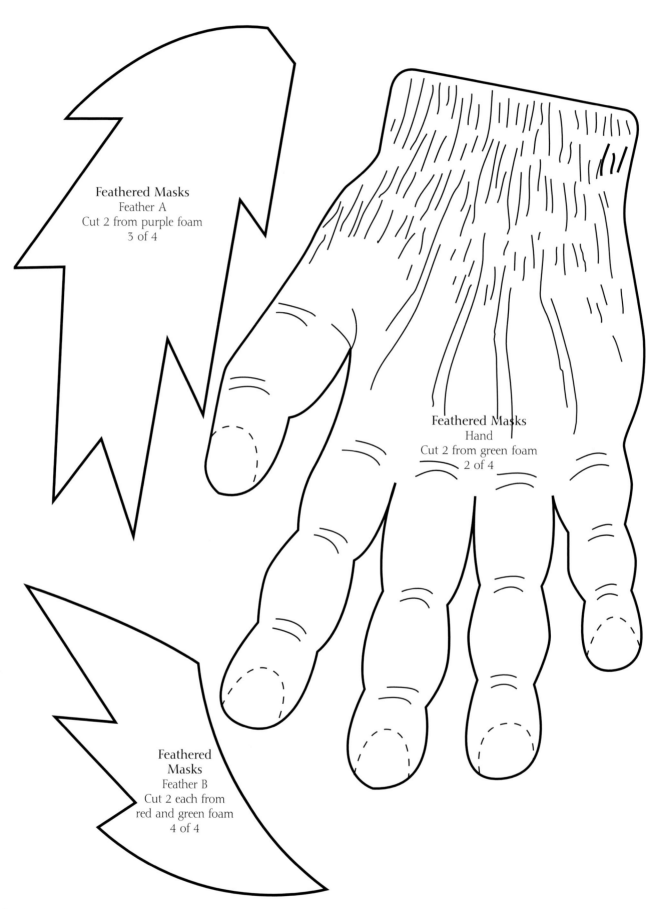

Feathered Masks
Feather A
Cut 2 from purple foam
3 of 4

Feathered Masks
Hand
Cut 2 from green foam
2 of 4

Feathered
Masks
Feather B
Cut 2 each from
red and green foam
4 of 4

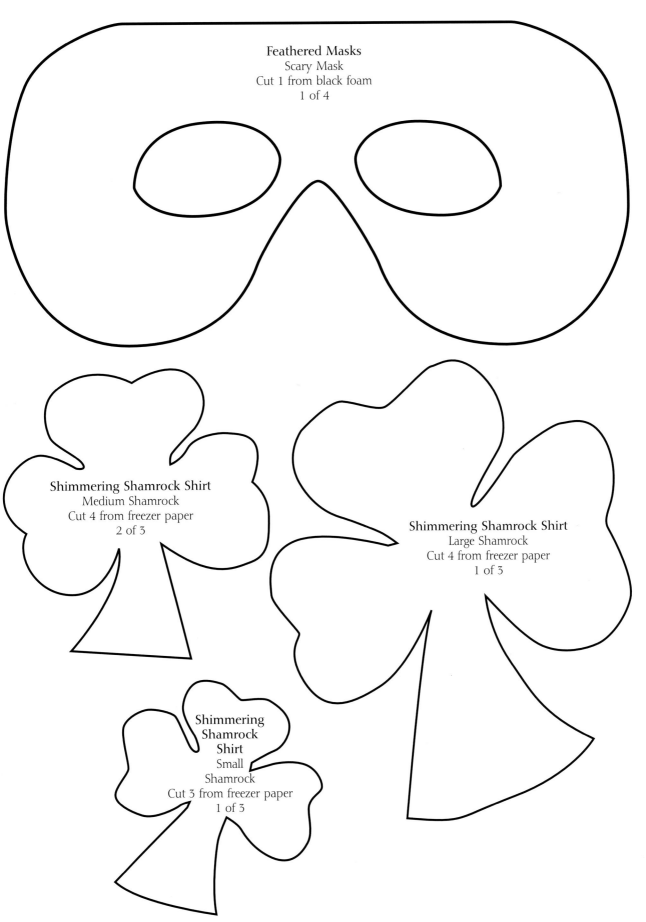

Feathered Masks
Scary Mask
Cut 1 from black foam
1 of 4

Shimmering Shamrock Shirt
Medium Shamrock
Cut 4 from freezer paper
2 of 3

Shimmering Shamrock Shirt
Large Shamrock
Cut 4 from freezer paper
1 of 3

Shimmering
Shamrock
Shirt
Small
Shamrock
Cut 3 from freezer paper
1 of 3

167

Nose
Cut 1 from fused black fabric
3 of 8

Nose/Eye
Cut 6 from fused black fabric
5 of 8

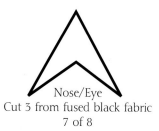

Nose/Eye
Cut 3 from fused black fabric
7 of 8

Faces of Halloween Quilt

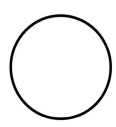

Mouth/Eye
Cut 3 from fused black fabric
4 of 8

Mouth
Cut 2 from fused black fabric
6 of 8

Mouth
Cut 2 from fused black fabric
8 of 8

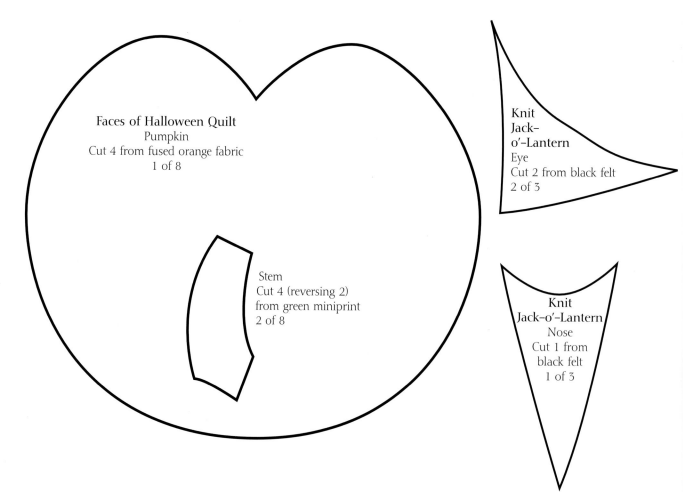

Faces of Halloween Quilt
Pumpkin
Cut 4 from fused orange fabric
1 of 8

Stem
Cut 4 (reversing 2)
from green miniprint
2 of 8

Knit
Jack–o'–Lantern
Eye
Cut 2 from black felt
2 of 3

Knit
Jack-o'-Lantern
Nose
Cut 1 from
black felt
1 of 3

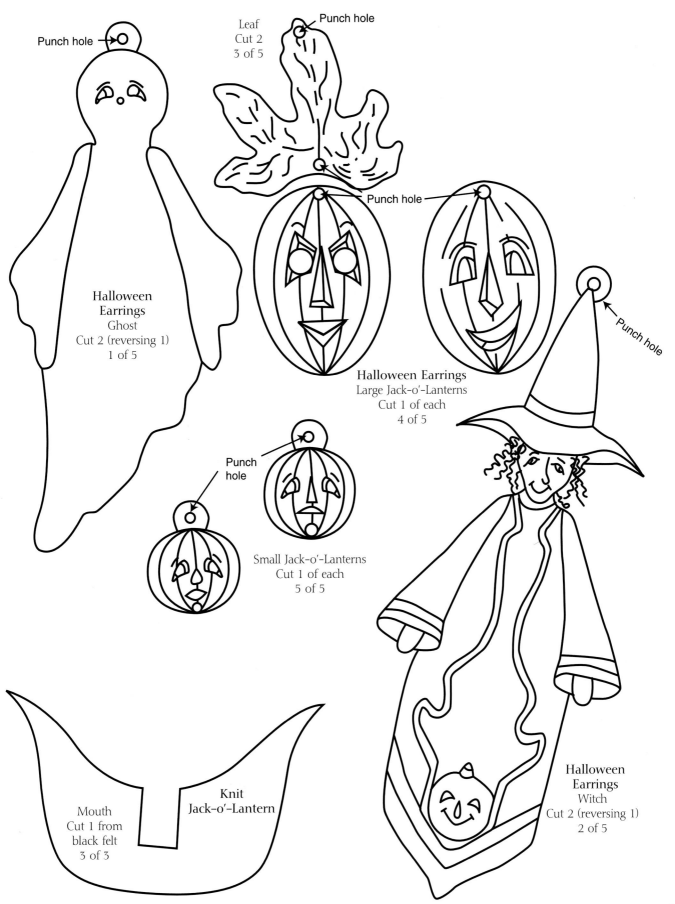

Punch hole →

Halloween
Earrings
Ghost
Cut 2 (reversing 1)
1 of 5

Leaf
Cut 2
3 of 5

Punch hole →

Punch hole

Halloween Earrings
Large Jack-o'-Lanterns
Cut 1 of each
4 of 5

Punch hole →

Punch
hole

Small Jack-o'-Lanterns
Cut 1 of each
5 of 5

Punch hole

Halloween
Earrings
Witch
Cut 2 (reversing 1)
2 of 5

Mouth
Cut 1 from
black felt
3 of 3

Knit
Jack-o'-Lantern

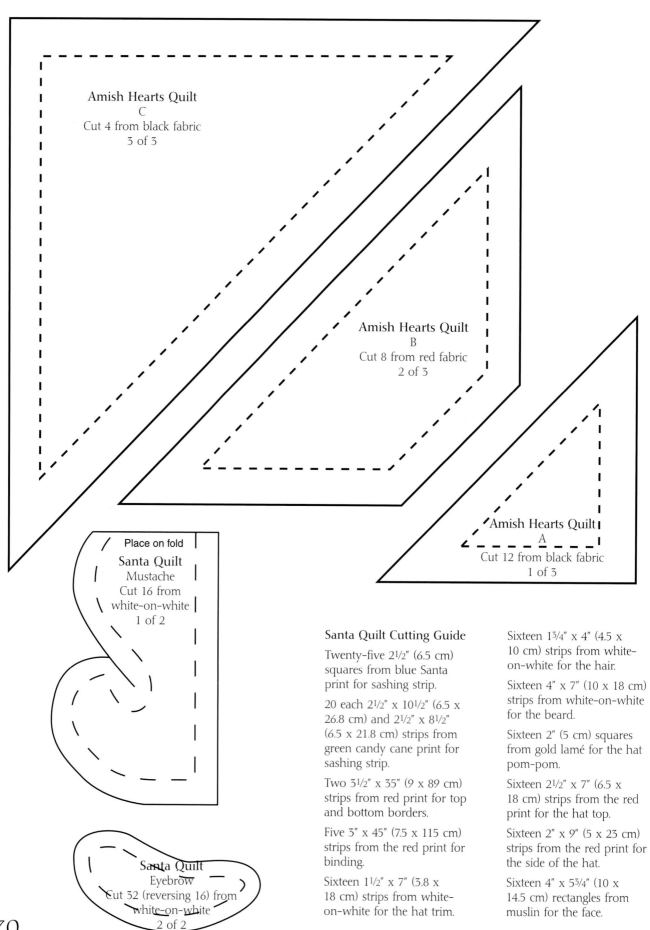

Amish Hearts Quilt
C
Cut 4 from black fabric
3 of 3

Amish Hearts Quilt
B
Cut 8 from red fabric
2 of 3

Amish Hearts Quilt
A
Cut 12 from black fabric
1 of 3

Place on fold

Santa Quilt
Mustache
Cut 16 from
white-on-white
1 of 2

Santa Quilt
Eyebrow
Cut 32 (reversing 16) from
white-on-white
2 of 2

Santa Quilt Cutting Guide

Twenty-five 2½" (6.5 cm) squares from blue Santa print for sashing strip.

20 each 2½" x 10½" (6.5 x 26.8 cm) and 2½" x 8½" (6.5 x 21.8 cm) strips from green candy cane print for sashing strip.

Two 3½" x 35" (9 x 89 cm) strips from red print for top and bottom borders.

Five 3" x 45" (7.5 x 115 cm) strips from the red print for binding.

Sixteen 1½" x 7" (3.8 x 18 cm) strips from white-on-white for the hat trim.

Sixteen 1¾" x 4" (4.5 x 10 cm) strips from white-on-white for the hair.

Sixteen 4" x 7" (10 x 18 cm) strips from white-on-white for the beard.

Sixteen 2" (5 cm) squares from gold lamé for the hat pom-pom.

Sixteen 2½" x 7" (6.5 x 18 cm) strips from the red print for the hat top.

Sixteen 2" x 9" (5 x 23 cm) strips from the red print for the side of the hat.

Sixteen 4" x 5¾" (10 x 14.5 cm) rectangles from muslin for the face.

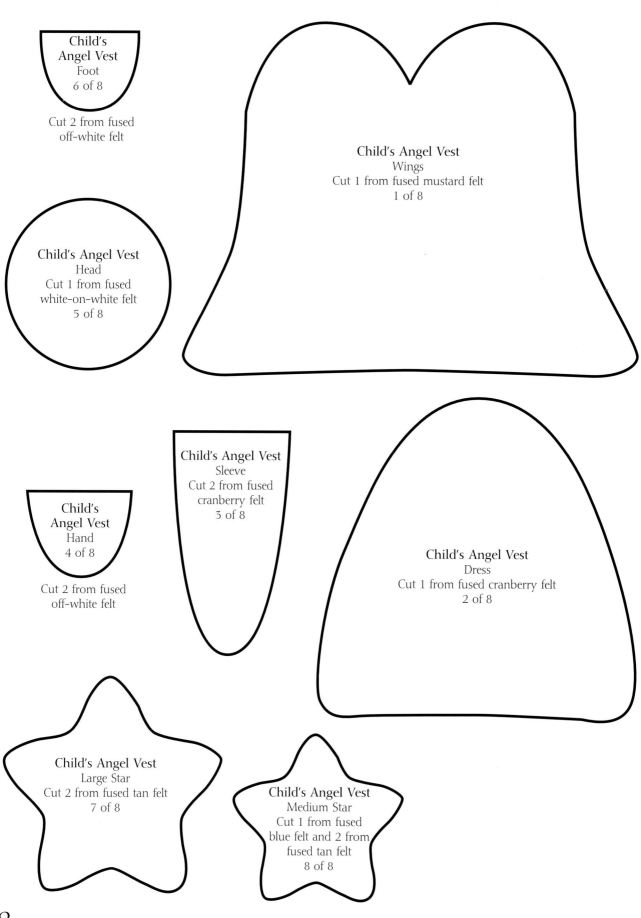

Child's
Angel Vest
Foot
6 of 8

Cut 2 from fused
off-white felt

Child's Angel Vest
Wings
Cut 1 from fused mustard felt
1 of 8

Child's Angel Vest
Head
Cut 1 from fused
white-on-white felt
5 of 8

Child's Angel Vest
Sleeve
Cut 2 from fused
cranberry felt
3 of 8

Child's
Angel Vest
Hand
4 of 8

Cut 2 from fused
off-white felt

Child's Angel Vest
Dress
Cut 1 from fused cranberry felt
2 of 8

Child's Angel Vest
Large Star
Cut 2 from fused tan felt
7 of 8

Child's Angel Vest
Medium Star
Cut 1 from fused
blue felt and 2 from
fused tan felt
8 of 8

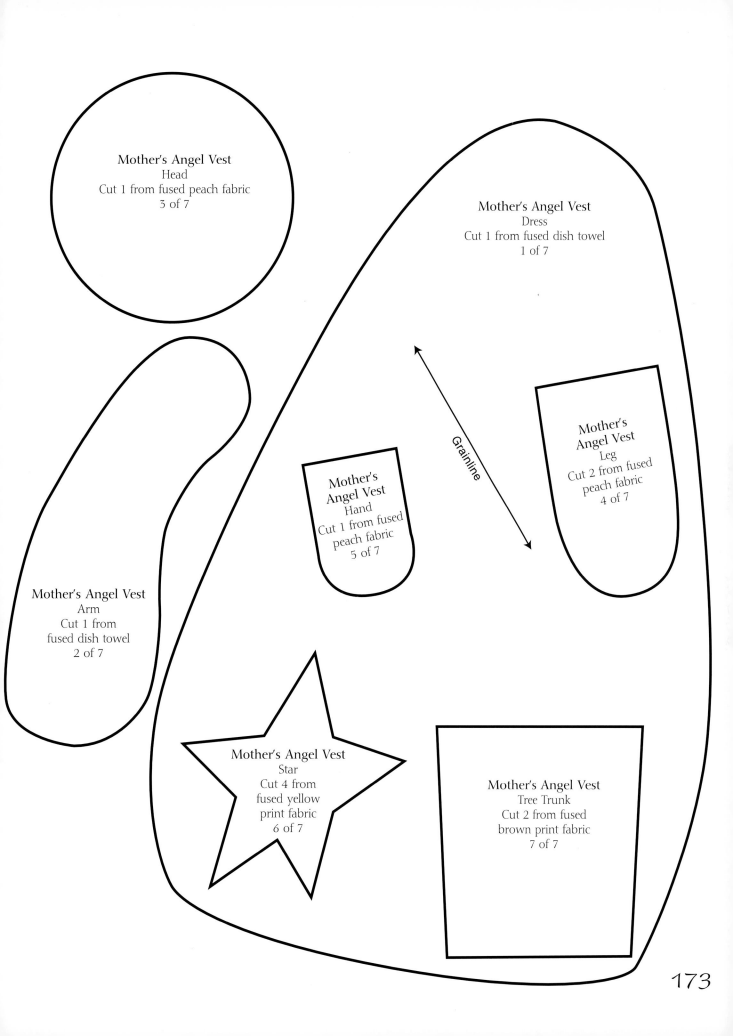

Mother's Angel Vest
Head
Cut 1 from fused peach fabric
3 of 7

Mother's Angel Vest
Dress
Cut 1 from fused dish towel
1 of 7

Grainline

Mother's
Angel Vest
Leg
Cut 2 from fused
peach fabric
4 of 7

Mother's
Angel Vest
Hand
Cut 1 from fused
peach fabric
5 of 7

Mother's Angel Vest
Arm
Cut 1 from
fused dish towel
2 of 7

Mother's Angel Vest
Star
Cut 4 from
fused yellow
print fabric
6 of 7

Mother's Angel Vest
Tree Trunk
Cut 2 from fused
brown print fabric
7 of 7

173

Copper Candle Holders
Maple Leaf
Trace 1
1 of 2

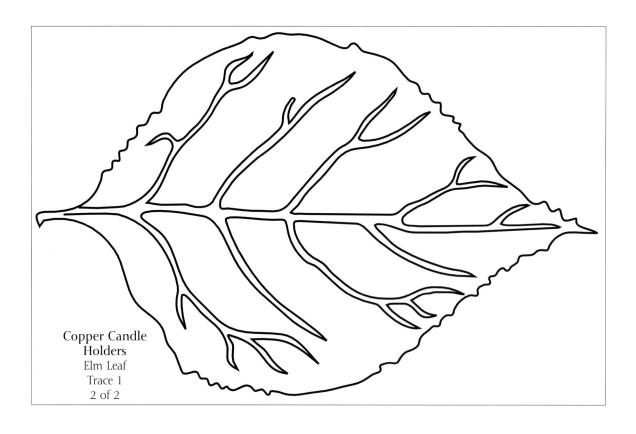

Copper Candle
Holders
Elm Leaf
Trace 1
2 of 2

Sources

Most of these items are available at your local craft retail stores. If you are having difficulties locating items, or live far from a retail store, please reference the sources listed below.

Page 4 *Year-Round Spheres:* Mexican Pottery Clay™ and molding tools are available from American Art Clay Co. Inc. Call 800-374-1600 for catalog.

Page 10 *Floral Shadow Box:* Walnut Hollow Keepsake Box #3211; call 800-950-5101 or write 1409 State Road 23, Dodgeville, WI 53533-2112. American Oak Preserving Co. dried florals; call 800-348-5008 or write 601 Mulberry St., North Judson, IN 46366.

Page 22 *Heart Smart Pinafore:* Wimpole Street dishtowels, Battenberg doily and yo yo. Wimpole Street Creations are available from Barrett House; call 801-299-0700 or write PO Box 540585, N. Salt Lake, UT 84054-0585.

Page 34 *Holiday Bunnies:* Wimpole Street bunnies, doilies and dishtowel fabric. Wimpole Street Creations are available from Barrett House; call 801-299-0700 or write PO Box 540585, N. Salt Lake, UT 84054-0585.

Page 42 *Passover or Easter Table Settings:* Charles Craft Royal Classic placemat and napkin; call 910-844-3521 or 800-277-0980, or write PO Box 1049; Laurinburg, NC 28353.

Page 48 *Church in the Valley:* Walnut Hollow Large Cloud Cabin #11106; call 800-950-5101 or write 1409 State Road 23, Dodgeville, WI 53533-2112.

Page 68 *Springtime Lamb:* Wimpole Street lamb, tea towel and doily. Wimpole Street Creations are available from Barrett House; call 801-299-0700 or write PO Box 540585, N. Salt Lake, UT 84054-0585.

Page 88 *Pamper Your Parents:* Soaps, oils, fragrances, soap molds and other ingredients are available from Victorian Essences; www.VictorianEssence.com, or call 888-446-5455 or write PO Box 1220, Arcadia, CA 91077.

Page 92 *Americana Wood Quilt:* Forster Woodsies™ Too squares and stars. Forster Woodsies are available from Alpine Imports; call 800-654-6114 or write 7106 N. Alpine Rd., Rockford, IL 61111.

Page 96 *American Comet Topper:* Call National Nonwovens at 800-333-3469 ext. 214 for retailers who carry WoolFelt® by the yard. Royal Blue 572, white 1100, red 938, gold 416.

Page 102 *Popsicle Stick Uncle Sam:* Forster regular and jumbo craft sticks. Forster Woodsies are available from Alpine Imports; call 800-654-6114 or write 7106 N. Alpine Rd., Rockford, IL 61111.

Page 106 *Mitten & Glove Witches:* Wimpole Street mitten, gloves, Battenberg doilies and dishtowel fabric. Wimpole Street Creations are available from Barrett House; call 801-299-0700 or write PO Box 540585, N. Salt Lake, UT 84054-0585.

Page 130 *Harvest of Plenty:* Walnut Hollow Rectangle Tray #3575, 24-color oil pencil set #9924 and transfer paper #1095; call 800-950-5101 or write 1409 State Road 23, Dodgeville, WI 53533-2112.

Page 142 *Hanukkah Sampler & Table Setting:* Charles Craft Royal Classic placemat, napkin and breadcover; call 910-844-3521 or 800-277-0980, or write PO Box 1049; Laurinburg, NC 28353. Provided by DMC, their embroidery floss and metallic thread were used.

Page 152 *Craft Stick Nativity Ornament:* Forster Woodsies™ squares and stars. Forster Woodsies are available from Alpine Imports; call 800-654-6114 or write 7106 N. Alpine Rd., Rockford, IL 61111.

Credits

Thanks to the following manufacturers for donating these craft projects for publication purposes.

Page 4 *Jeweled Heart Pin*
Provided by Westrim® Crafts; their beads, mounted jewels and gold cord were used.

Page 26 *Amish Hearts Quilt*
Provided by Dow Chemical Co.; their Styrofoam® was used.

Page 72 *Tee Time Clock*
Provided by Delta; their Ceramcoat® waterbase sealer, acrylic paints, Baroque Bronze glazing kit, acrylic satin varnish, Stencil Magic® Stencil Adhesive Spray and Wood Wiz® wood glue were used.

Page 94 *Fourth of July Napkins & Holder*
Provided by Delta; their Ceramcoat® acrylic paints and exterior varnish were used.

Page 100 *Star-Spangled T-Shirts*
Provided by Duncan; their Scribbles® 3 Dimensional Fabric Writers and Brush 'n' Soft fabric paint were used.

Page 104 *Candy Corn Clay Pots*
Provided by Aleene's; their Premium–Coat™ acrylic paints, Gloss Varnish and Sharpie marker were used.

Page 112 *Feathered Masks*
Provided by Zucker; their peacock feathers were used.

Page 114 *Knit Jack-o'-Lantern*
Provided by Coats and Clark; their Red Heart yarn was used.